ESSENTIAL ELEMENTS
FOR GUITAR

COMPREHENSIVE GUITAR METHOD
WILL SCHMID   BOB MORRIS

Learning to play guitar will bring you a lifetime of enjoyment. Guitar can be your window to a wide variety of musical styles including rock, jazz, country, blues, folk, classical, and many more. It can become your solo instrument or be used in ensemble with other players. For many, the guitar is also a source of accompaniment to songs—perhaps even some that you, yourself, compose. Have fun, and practice, practice, practice.

—Will Schmid and Bob Morris

The guitar has its roots in the ancient Near East. In Babylonia and Egypt, examples of art show stringed instruments with necks that resemble the guitar. The Moors (Muslims of Arab and North African descent) brought ancestors of the modern guitar into Spain during the period from the 8th to the 15th centuries. In other parts of the world, relatives of the guitar (China: *pipa*; Japan: *biwa*; India: *sitar*; Russia: *balalaika*) were developed at about the same time. In 16th-century Spain, the two most popular fretted instruments were the *vihuela* (which ended up with six double-gut strings and 12 frets) and the lute (the pear-shaped favorite). By the end of the Baroque period (1600–1750), the guitar had become a smaller, narrow-bodied, six-string version of what we know today. During the next hundred years, composer/performers such as Sor, Guilliani, Carcassi, and Carulli wrote both methods and solos for the instrument. The violin virtuoso, Paganini, was also an accomplished guitarist. Around 1850, Antonio de Torres reworked the design and construction of the classical guitar, and his designs are still used today.

In the United States, three different companies—Martin, Gibson, and Fender—spearheaded the development of steel-string and electric guitars. C.F. Martin & Co., famous for their dreadnought steel-string guitars (1931), was established in 1833 in New York City, moving shortly thereafter to Nazareth, PA. Gibson Guitars, famous for their archtop, f-hole models and Les Paul electrics, was started in the 1880s in Kalamazoo, MI. Gibson's Lloyd Loar began experimenting with electric pickups in hollowbody guitars as early as the 1920s. By 1951, Leo Fender had invented the first solidbody electric guitar that would eventually be the Fender Telecaster®, and the electric bass followed shortly. Today, a wide variety of companies are producing new types of guitars such as acoustic-electrics, MIDI guitars, and the silhouette-body Silent Guitar® that are used in conjunction with amplifiers and effects devices.

HISTORY OF THE GUITAR

ISBN-13: 978-1-4234-5362-8
ISBN-10: 1-4234-5362-X

HAL•LEONARD®
CORPORATION
7777 W. BLUEMOUND RD. P.O. BOX 13819 MILWAUKEE, WI 53213

GETTING STARTED

Rest Position

It is important to keep the guitar silent when the teacher is speaking to the class.

Follow the directions below when instructed to go to the Rest Position.

- Lay the guitar flat across your lap with the strings facing down.
- Lay your hands on the back of the guitar.
- Stay quiet and still until the teacher asks you to go to the Playing Position.

Playing Position

There are several ways to hold the guitar comfortably. Pictured here are two typical seated positions. Observe the following general guidelines in forming your playing posture.

- Position your body, arms, and legs in such a way that you avoid tension.
- If you feel tension creeping into your playing, you probably need to reassess your position.
- Tilt the neck of the guitar slightly upwards—never down.
- Avoid slanting the top of the guitar so that you can see better. Balance your weight evenly from left to right. Sit straight (but not rigid).

Tuning

Tuning means setting the correct pitch (highness or lowness of sound) of each string. To tune your guitar, you will adjust the pitch of each string by turning the corresponding tuning key on the head of the instrument. Tightening a string raises a pitch, and loosening it lowers the pitch. See page 92 for different tuning methods.

The strings are numbered 1 through 6 beginning with the thinnest string (the one closest to your knee). Tune each string in sequence by listening to the correct pitch and slowly turning the tuning key until the sound of the string matches the pitch.

YOUR GUITAR

This book is designed for use with any type of guitar—acoustic or electric. Any of these guitars can be adapted for use in a wide variety of styles of music. Take some time getting familiar with the individual parts of your guitar as shown on this page.

ACOUSTIC
Steel-String

Nylon-String (Classical)

ELECTRIC

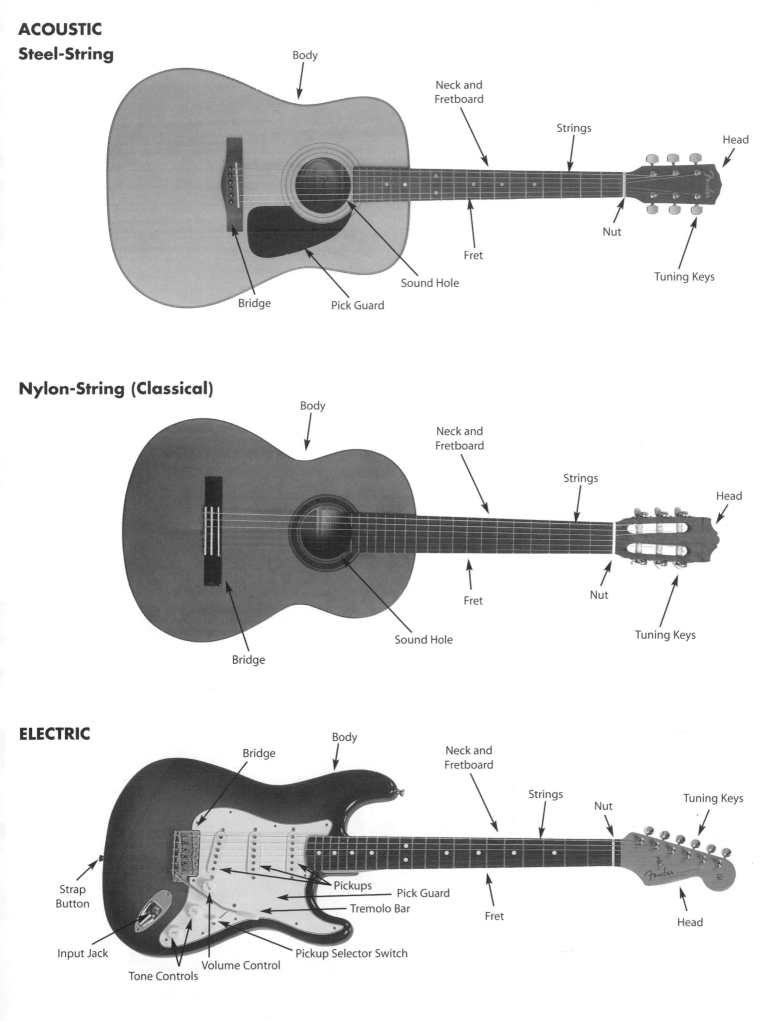

PLAYING CHORDS

Left-Hand Position

Left-hand fingers are numbered 1 through 4. (Pianists: Note that the thumb is **not** number 1.) Place your thumb on the underside of the guitar neck and arch your fingers over the fingerboard. Position your thumb roughly the opposite of your 2nd finger. Avoid touching the guitar neck with your palm.

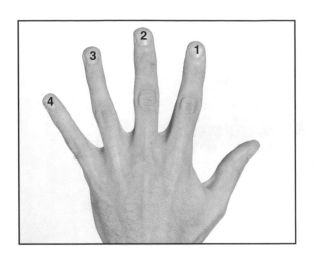
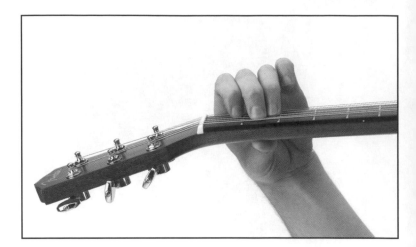

Right-Hand Position

When you play, you'll be striking the strings with either your thumb or with a pick held in your right hand. To hold the pick properly, grip it between your thumb and index finger.

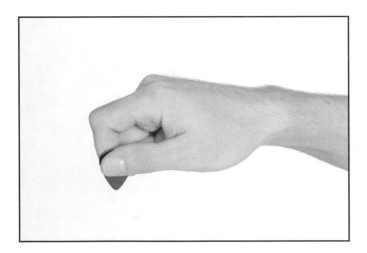

Chords & The Chord Diagram

A chord is sounded when three or more strings are played at the same time. Your first two chords will be the C and G7 chords. Begin by looking at the chord diagram below to understand how these chords will be played. An "O" shown above a string indicates that the string should be played "open," or without a finger on the string. An "X" indicates that the string should not be played. Memorize the parts of the chord diagram including string numbers and letter names.

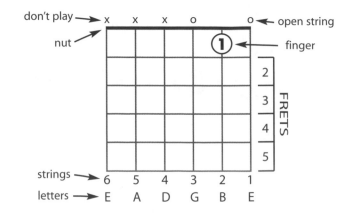

PLAYING CHORDS

Study the photos and diagrams below to begin playing chords. Depress the string indicated with the tip of your 1st finger. Arch your finger to avoid touching strings that are to be played open. With your right hand holding the pick over the soundhole, strum across strings 3 through 1 in a downward motion. Or you may strum the strings with your thumb. The full versions of the C and G7 chords can be found on pages 23 and 25, respectively.

C Chord

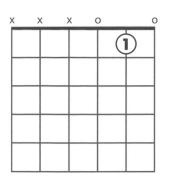

G7 Chord

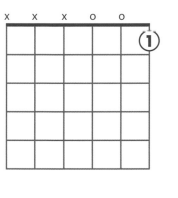

STRUM BUILDER 1

When the chords are used as accompaniment to singing, they must be strummed with a steady, even stroke. Practice the following exercises by strumming once for each slash mark (╱), and changing chords when indicated above the slashes. Repeat the patterns several times while focusing on playing clear and evenly spaced chords.

1. A PERFECT PAIR

C   G7

╱ ╱ ╱ ╱ ╱ ╱ ╱ ╱ ╱ ╱ ╱ ╱ ╱ ╱ ╱ ╱

2. ROLLING ALONG

C   G7   C   G7   C

╱ ╱ ╱ ╱ ╱ ╱ ╱ ╱ ╱ ╱ ╱ ╱ ╱ ╱ ╱ ╱

PLAYING CHORDS

Beat = The *Pulse* of Music

The **beat** of music should be very steady, just like your pulse.

Quarter Note ♩ **= 1 Beat of Sound**

Notes tell us how high or low to play, and how long to play.

Music Staff

The **music staff** has 5 lines and 4 spaces.

Music Staff → | *Measure* | *Measure* |

Bar Lines

Bar lines divide the music staff into **measures**.

Bar Line   *Bar Line*   *Bar Line*

Measures

The **measures** on this page have four beats each.

Now let's try strumming the C chord and singing a tune. The teacher should sing the melody for the class the first time through and then the class is encouraged to join in. Follow the slashes above the music staff for strumming. Read the music from left to right, as you would read words in a book. Don't worry about the music symbols you haven't seen yet, just sing along with your teacher. Soon you'll learn more about what they mean.

3. ARE YOU STRUMMING?

Are you strum-ming? Are you strum-ming? Yes I am. Yes I am.

I am a gui-tar-ist. I am a gui-tar-ist. Watch me jam. Watch me jam.

Time Signature (Meter)

4 = 4 beats per measure
4 = ♩ gets one beat

The **time signature** tells us how many beats are in each measure and what kind of note gets one beat.

Double Bar

A **double bar** indicates the end of a piece of music or a transition within the music.

PLAYING CHORDS

Now let's try strumming and singing your first two songs.

4. HE'S GOT THE WHOLE WORLD IN HIS HANDS

Repeat Sign 𝄇   Without stopping, play once again from the previous **repeat sign**.

THEORY

5. WATER COME A ME EYE

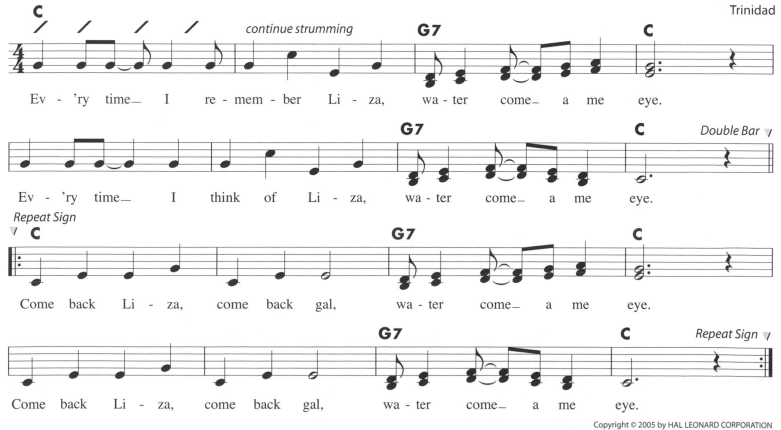

COUNTING

THEORY

Counting Count **1 & 2 & 3 & 4 &**   One beat = Tap toe down on the number and up on "&."
          Tap ↓ ↑ ↓ ↑ ↓ ↑ ↓ ↑   Always count when playing.

Half Note   **Whole Note**

= 2 Beats   = 4 Beats

1 & 2 &   1 & 2 & 3 & 4 &

6. THE CLAPPER *Clap the rhythm while counting.*

Clap

Count 1 2 3 4 1 2 3 4 1 2 3 4 1 2 3 4 1 2 3 4 1 2 3 4

7. TAP 'N' PICK *Pick the open first string in the rhythm shown while tapping the beats with your toe.*

Pick

Tap 1 2 3 4 1 2 3 4 1 2 3 4 1 2 3 4 1 2 3 4 1 2 3 4

8. THE WHOLE NINE YARDS *Pick the open first string in the rhythm shown while tapping the beats.*

Pick

Tap 1 2 3 4 1 2 3 4 1 2 3 4 1 2 3 4 1 2 3 4 1 2 3 4

9. ESSENTIAL ELEMENTS QUIZ *Write in the number of beats that each note lasts.*

4

___ ___ ___ ___ ___ ___ ___ ___ ___ ___ ___

THEORY

Treble Clef   Lines   Spaces

E G B D F   F A C E

Clefs indicate a set of note names.

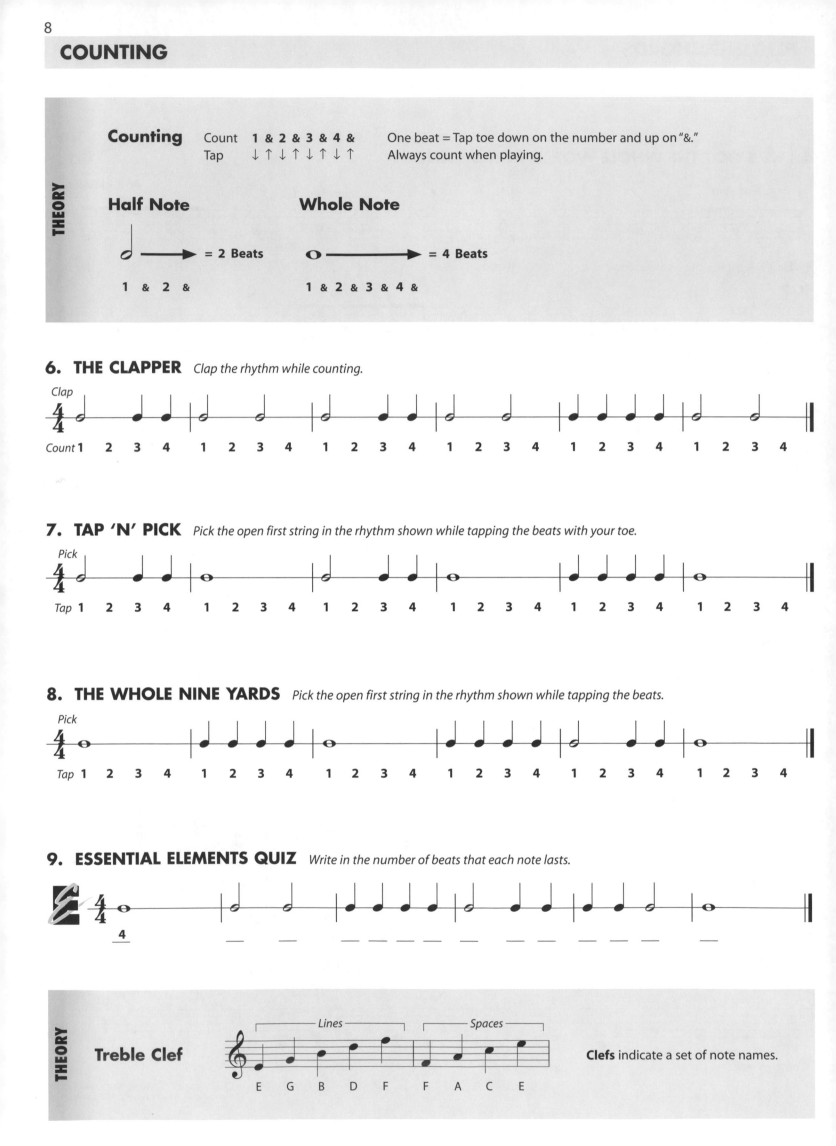

9

NOTES ON THE FIRST STRING

Now let's play some single notes. Follow the same right- and left-hand position guidelines as you did with chords. Here you will pick only one string at a time.

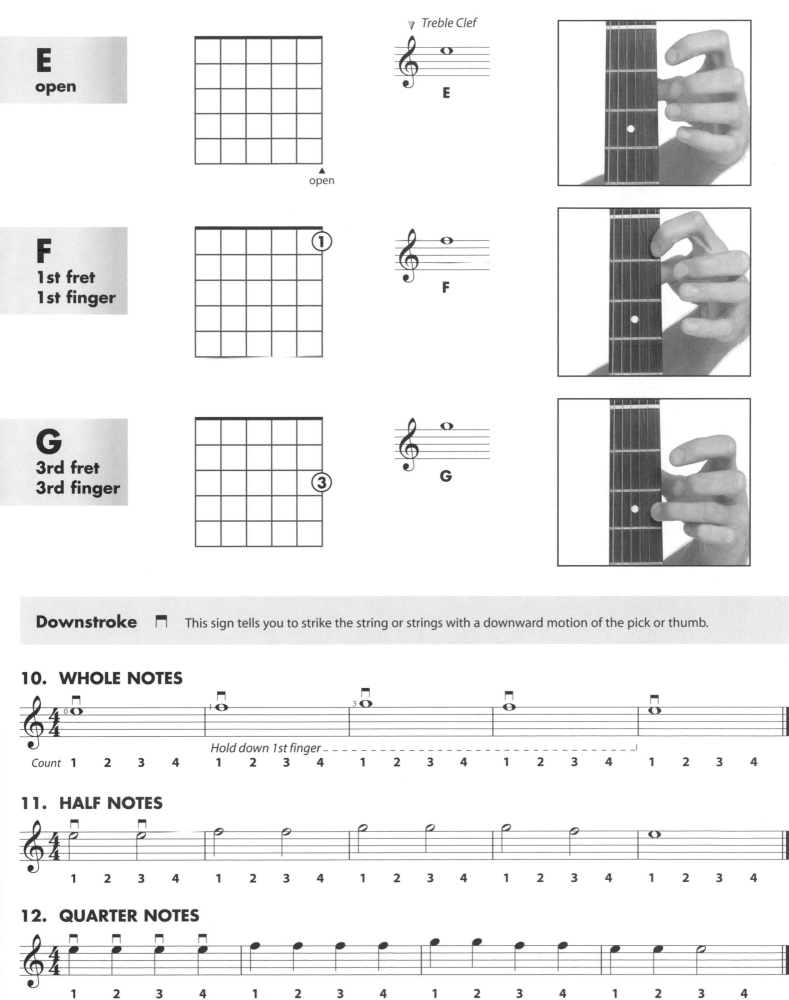

Downstroke ⊓ This sign tells you to strike the string or strings with a downward motion of the pick or thumb.

10. WHOLE NOTES

Count 1   2   3   4   1   2   3   4   1   2   3   4   1   2   3   4   1   2   3   4

Hold down 1st finger

11. HALF NOTES

1   2   3   4   1   2   3   4   1   2   3   4   1   2   3   4   1   2   3   4

12. QUARTER NOTES

1   2   3   4   1   2   3   4   1   2   3   4   1   2   3   4

NOTES ON THE FIRST STRING

At first practice the exercises slowly and steadily. When you can play them well at a slow speed, gradually increase the *tempo*, or speed.

13. BACK AND FORTH

14. SINGLE STRING THING *Touch only the tips of your fingers on the strings.*

15. TECHNIQUE TRAX *Keep your left-hand fingers arched over the strings.*

When you can play the melody successfully on the following tune, try adding the chords with a friend.

16. LINE TO LINE

17. SPANISH THEME *Spanish flamenco guitarists play this theme for dancing.*

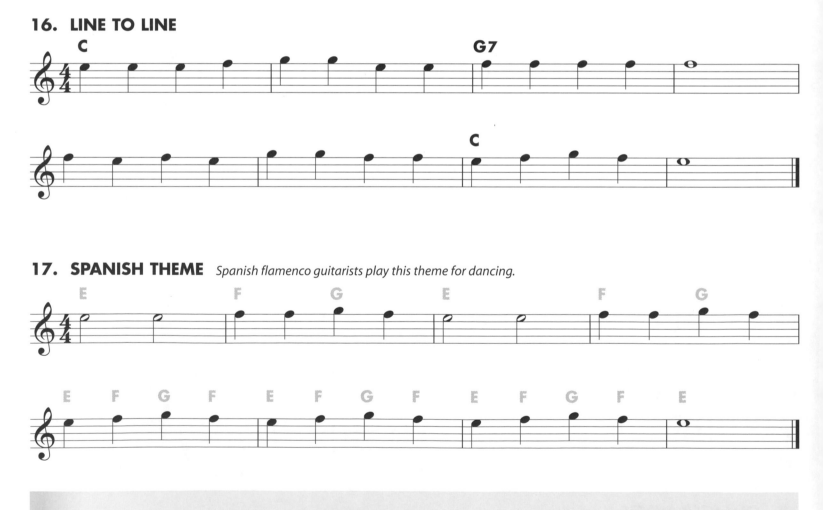

PLAYING CHORDS

Try these two new chords: G and D7. Notice that the previous chords you've learned involve only three strings, as does the G chord introduced here. Later in the book, the full versions of these chords will be introduced. However, the D7 chord below is your first full chord, played with four strings. The full version of the G chord can be found on page 23.

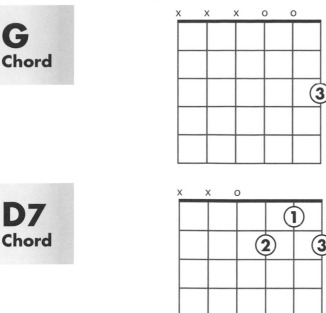

G Chord

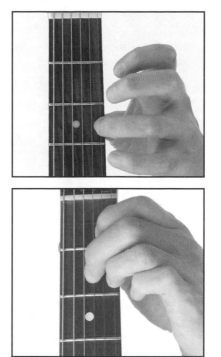

D7 Chord

When changing between the G and D7 chords, notice that the 3rd finger slides back and forth between the second and third fret on the first string.

18. CHORD PRACTICE *Strum the new chords once for each slash mark.*

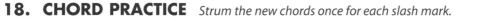

19. PAY ME MY MONEY DOWN *Strum the new chords while your teacher sings. Then join in singing as a class.*

PLAYING CHORDS

HISTORY

Hank Williams (1923–1953) was one of country music's best songwriters. "Jambalaya (On the Bayou)," set in a Louisiana Cajun style, is a lively two-chord song. A *bayou* is a term for a Louisiana swamp, where a *pirogue*, or canoe, is used to find *crawfish,* an ingredient in the delicious *jambalaya* recipe.

Try strumming the chords to this song without the slashes. Just follow the chord symbols as the song progresses. Use the same strum pattern as before. Remember there are four beats in each measure.

20. JAMBALAYA (ON THE BAYOU)

21. ESSENTIAL ELEMENTS QUIZ
Play the chord exercise below for your teacher. Strum once for each slash and change chords when indicated.

NOTES ON THE SECOND STRING

Next, play these new single notes. Notice that they are played in exactly the same way as the notes you've learned on the first string, only now on the second string.

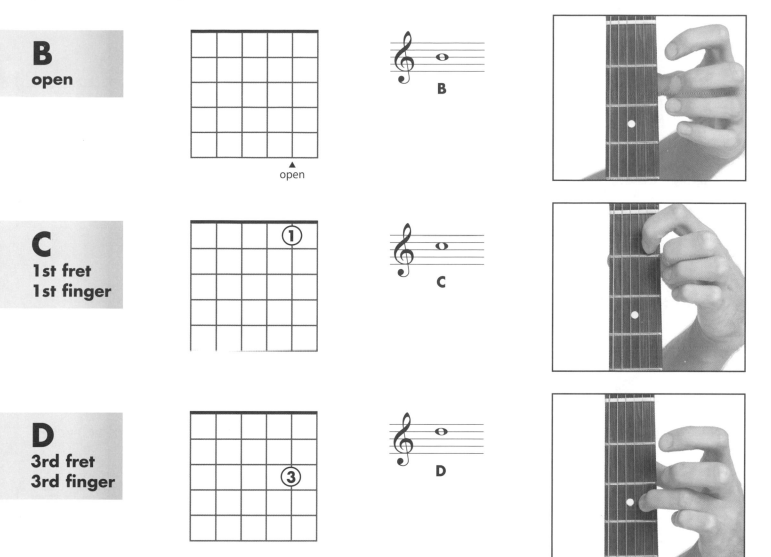

B
open

C
1st fret
1st finger

D
3rd fret
3rd finger

Try the new notes in the exercises below. Remember to pick each note with downstrokes (⊓). Focus on picking only the second string, being careful to avoid the neighboring strings.

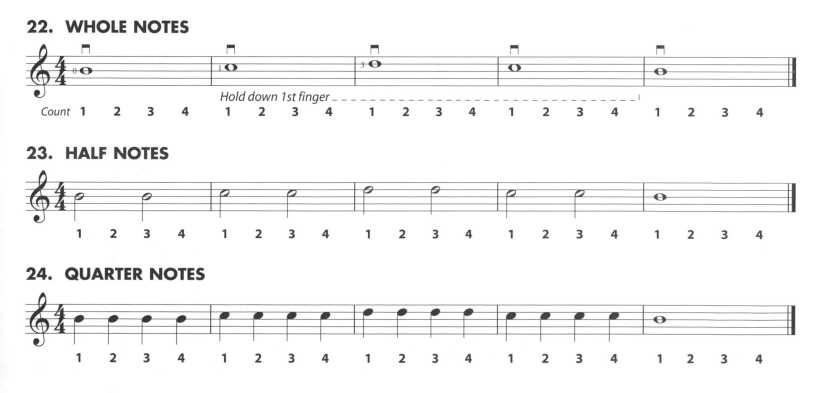

22. WHOLE NOTES

Count 1 2 3 4   1 2 3 4   1 2 3 4   1 2 3 4   1 2 3 4

Hold down 1st finger

23. HALF NOTES

1 2 3 4   1 2 3 4   1 2 3 4   1 2 3 4   1 2 3 4

24. QUARTER NOTES

1 2 3 4   1 2 3 4   1 2 3 4   1 2 3 4   1 2 3 4

NOTES ON THE SECOND STRING

Always practice the exercises slowly and steadily at first. After you can play them well at a slower tempo, gradually increase the speed. If some of your notes are fuzzy or unclear, adjust your left-hand finger slightly until you hear a clear sound.

25. OVER AND UNDER THE SEA

26. TWO OF A KIND

27. SECOND HELPING

You have learned six notes now, three on the first string and three on the second string. In the following exercises you will be moving from string to string. As you are playing one note, look ahead to the next and get your fingers in position.

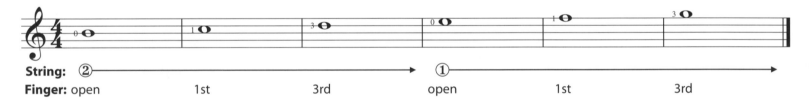

String: ② → ① →
Finger: open   1st   3rd   open   1st   3rd

28. CROSSING OVER

29. WILD STRINGDOM

PLAYING CHORDS

Pick-Up Notes One or more notes that come before the first *full* measure of a song. When a song begins with **pick-up notes**, the last measure will be short the exact number of beats used as pick-ups.

The next two songs contain three of the chords you have learned so far. After you feel comfortable playing the chords, try singing *and* playing the chords. Notice the pick-up notes in the first partial measure of the song. Sing the first words, "This land is…," then begin strumming the steady beat where you see the C chord symbol. Additional verses are listed below the song; just follow the chord names shown above the words as you continue strumming and singing the same melody.

30. THIS LAND IS YOUR LAND

TRO - © Copyright 1956 (Renewed), 1958 (Renewed), 1970 (Renewed) and 1972 (Renewed) Ludlow Music, Inc., New York, NY
International Copyright Secured
All Rights Reserved Including Public Performance For Profit
Used by Permission

1.
    C   **G**
As I was walking that ribbon of highway

    D7   **G**
I saw above me that endless skyway;

    C   **G**
I saw below me that golden valley;

D7   **G**
This land was made for you and me.

To Chorus

2.
    C   **G**
I've roamed and rambled and I followed my footsteps;

    D7   **G**
To the sparkling sands of her diamond deserts;

    C   **G**
And all around me a voice was sounding;

D7   **G**
This land was made for you and me.

To Chorus

PLAYING CHORDS

HISTORY

Robert Johnson (1889–1938) was the best known of the country blues guitarists from the Mississippi Delta. His popularity was on the rise around the same time that Woody Guthrie was traveling the country and singing his own songs. Johnson's signature tune, "Crossroad Blues," has been played by many guitarists, including Eric Clapton.

31. SWEET HOME CHICAGO

Robert Johnson

Come on, ba - by don't-cha wan - na go? Come on,

ba - by don't-cha wan - na go? Back to that

same old place, sweet home Chi - ca - go?

1. One and one is two, six and two are eight, come on ba - by don't-cha
2. Six and three are nine, nine and nine eight - een, come on ba - by can't-cha

make me late! / Hey, ba - by don't-cha wan - na go?
see what I mean. \

Back to that same old place, sweet home Chi - ca - go?

PLAYING SINGLE NOTES

German composer **Ludwig van Beethoven** (1770–1827) is considered to be one of the world's greatest composers, despite becoming completely deaf in 1802. Although he could not hear his music the way we can, he could "hear" it in his mind. As a testament to his greatness, his *Symphony No. 9* was performed as the finale to the ceremony celebrating the reunification of Germany in 1990.

HISTORY

Practice these songs played on strings 1 and 2. Always begin slowly and then gradually increase the tempo. Gray chord symbols are used occasionally throughout the book to indicate that the chords should be played by the instructor.

32. ODE TO JOY (from *Symphony No. 9*)

Ludwig van Beethoven

33. BLUES

Blues is an African-American style of music that has roots going back hundreds of years. An early form of the blues that we know today began shortly after 1900 in the Mississippi Delta. It then spread north to Memphis, Chicago, and other cities.

HISTORY

PLAYING CHORDS

STRUM BUILDER 2

Down-Up Stroke

So far you have been using only downstrokes (⊓). Now you will learn to play upstrokes (V) between each beat. The **down-up stroke** *subdivides*, or halves, the beat. Later in the book, you will learn to play eighth notes that do the same thing. The down-up stroke is notated like this:

Once you feel comfortable playing the basic down-up stroke above, try using it in "Jambalaya" (page 12) and "This Land is Your Land" (page 15).

Intro   Some songs have an **intro** (short for introduction) before the song starts. Often it consists of the band playing through the main chords of the song once or twice.

On this particular song the band plays an instrumental intro, followed by Elvis Presley singing "You ain't nothin' but a hound dog," then the full band enters. Try playing the intro below before adding it to the song.

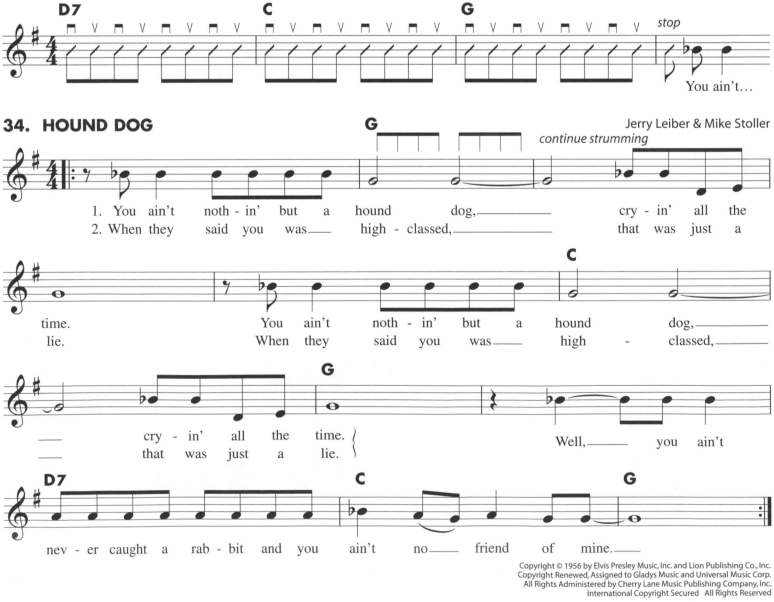

34. HOUND DOG

Jerry Leiber & Mike Stoller

PLAYING CHORDS

N.C. This symbol is short for "No Chord." This means no chord should be played whenever you see **N.C.** occur in the music.

This rock 'n' roll classic features all four chords you've learned so far.

35. ROCK AROUND THE CLOCK

Max C. Freedman & Jimmy DeKnight

One, two, three o'-clock, four o'-clock rock, five, six, sev-en o'-clock,

eight o'-clock rock, nine, ten, e-lev-en o'-clock, twelve o'-clock rock, we're gon-na

rock a-round the clock to-night.— 1. Put your glad rags on and join me, hon.— We'll
2. clock strikes two, and three and four,— if the

have some fun when the clock strikes one.— We're gon-na rock a-round the
band slows down we'll— yell for more.— We're gon-na rock a-round the

clock to-night,— we're gon-na rock, rock, rock, 'til broad day-light.— We're gon-na
clock to-night,— we're gon-na rock, rock, rock, 'til broad day-light.— We're gon-na

rock, gon-na rock a-round— the clock— to-night.—————— (2. When the)
rock, gon-na rock a-round— the clock— to-night.——————

Bill Haley & His Comets recorded "Rock Around the Clock" in 1955. This chart-topping hit, along with their smash "Shake, Rattle and Roll," was among the earliest rock 'n' roll tunes ever created.

HISTORY

PLAYING CHORDS

Chord Progression	The movement of one chord to the next, or a sequence of chords in a song.
Chord Changes	A term often used in jazz music meaning the chord progression of a song, or literally the changes from chord to chord.
Accompaniment	An instrument part that supports or is background to another part.

36. ESSENTIAL ELEMENTS QUIZ

Play through the chord changes below for your teacher. Strum using both the downstroke and the down-up stroke as indicated by the slash marks.

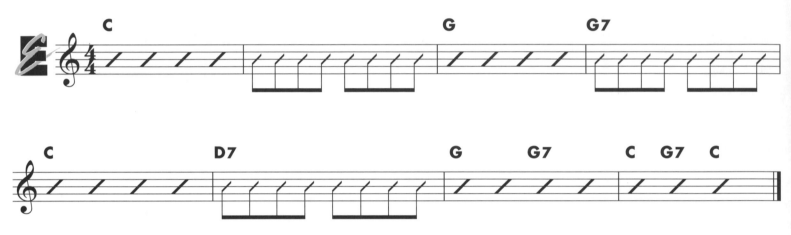

37. ESSENTIAL CREATIVITY

Using the four chords you've learned so far, create your own chord changes and play it for the teacher. Try using some of the different strum patterns that you've learned. Sing some words of your own as well for a little extra fun. You can write your song in the empty music staff provided below. Be sure to add in the proper music symbols.

NOTES ON THE THIRD STRING

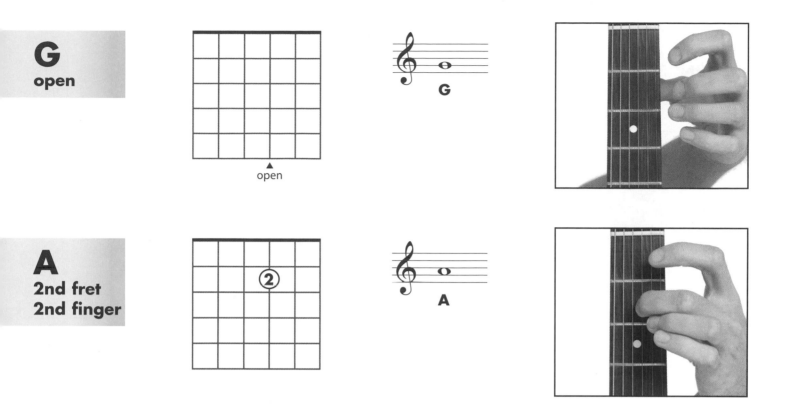

G
open

A
2nd fret
2nd finger

Keep the fingers arched over the strings at all times so they will be in position to finger the next note.

38. THIRD STRING WARM-UP

39. GUITAR GALLOP

STRING REVIEW

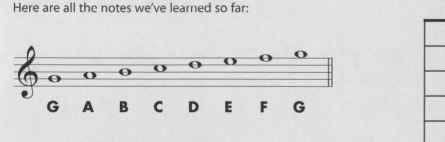

Here are all the notes we've learned so far:

G A B C D E F G

Play through these notes up and down. Listen closely to yourself and focus on crossing strings smoothly while producing clear, even tones. Listening carefully to your own playing is an essential element of creating music.

PLAYING SINGLE NOTES

The following songs use notes on strings 1, 2, and 3.

40. ROCKIN' ROBIN *Try strumming the chord progression as well.*

J. Thomas

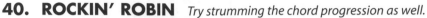

41. YANKEE DOODLE

Traditional

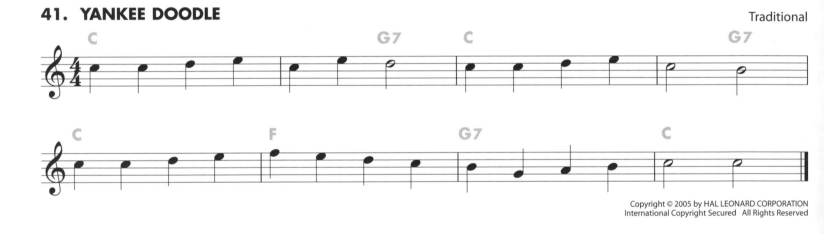

42. SURF ROCK *Play the chords once you've learned the melody.*

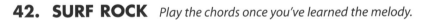

PLAYING CHORDS

The E minor chord (**Em**) is one of the easiest chords on the guitar. It is also your first chord using all six strings. Arch your fingers and play on the tips to avoid touching the other open strings.

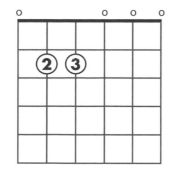

Now try out the full versions of the C and G chords.

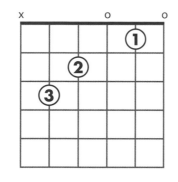

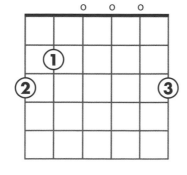

When you feel comfortable playing the E minor chord and the new C and G chords, try singing and strumming the next two songs.

PLAYING CHORDS

D.C. al Fine   At the **D.C. al Fine** play again from the beginning, stopping at **Fine** (fee-nay). **D.C.** is the abbreviation for Da Capo, or "to the head," and **Fine** means "the end."

STRUM BUILDER 3

After you have played through "Eleanor Rigby" using a simple downstroke on each beat, try this new variation on the down-up stroke. Let the first-beat strum ring for a full beat. Follow with the down (⊓) and up (∨) strokes carefully:

43. ELEANOR RIGBY   *Play the repeats until you've sung all three verses, then take the D.C. al Fine.*   John Lennon & Paul McCartney

HISTORY

John Lennon and Paul McCartney of **The Beatles** collaborated on numerous number-one hits during the 1960s. They were part of the "British Invasion" of rock groups that influenced American popular music during that period.

PLAYING CHORDS

STRUM BUILDER 4

When you have played the chords to the previous songs using a simple strum and feel comfortable with your left-hand changes, go back and use the new variation of the down-up stroke as an accompaniment to previous songs in the book.

The song below will give you good practice at combining the E minor chord with the full version of the G chord you have learned.

44. TELL OL' BILL *Play the repeats three times, once for each of the three verses.*

Traditional

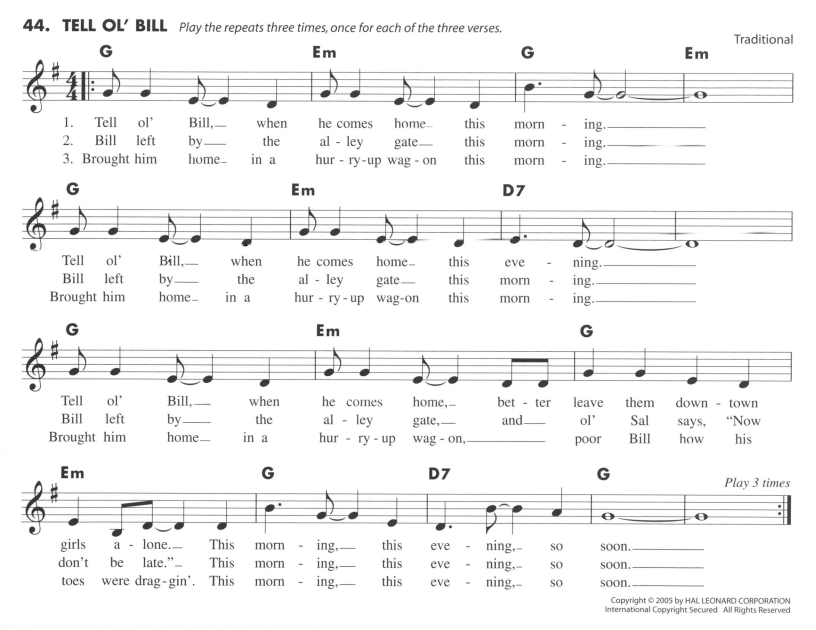

1. Tell ol' Bill,— when he comes home— this morn - ing.————
2. Bill left by— the al - ley gate— this morn - ing.————
3. Brought him home— in a hur - ry-up wag - on this morn - ing.————

Tell ol' Bill,— when he comes home— this eve - ning.————
Bill left by— the al - ley gate— this morn - ing.————
Brought him home— in a hur - ry-up wag-on this morn - ing.————

Tell ol' Bill,— when he comes home,— bet - ter leave them down - town
Bill left by— the al - ley gate,— and— ol' Sal says, "Now
Brought him home— in a hur - ry - up wag - on,———— poor Bill how his

Play 3 times

girls a - lone.— This morn - ing,— this eve - ning,– so soon.————
don't be late."— This morn - ing,— this eve - ning,– so soon.————
toes were drag - gin'. This morn - ing,— this eve - ning,– so soon.————

Next, try out the full version of the G7 chord. Notice how easy it is to change between this chord and the C chord. Go back to page 5 and play exercises 1 and 2 (in Strum Builder 1) with the full G7 and C chords. Also play them with "He's Got the Whole World in His Hands" and "Water Come a Me Eye" (page 7).

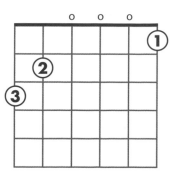

G7 Chord

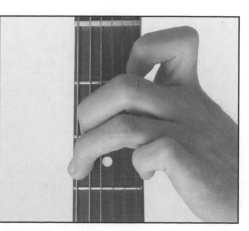

PERFORMANCE SPOTLIGHT

Duet   A song that has two different parts that can be played together.

Practice both parts of the following duet. Ask your instructor or a friend to play the duet along with you. Also try playing the chord accompaniment while others play the part(s).

45. AU CLAIR DE LA LUNE

France

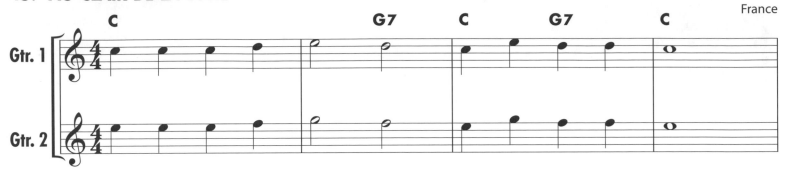

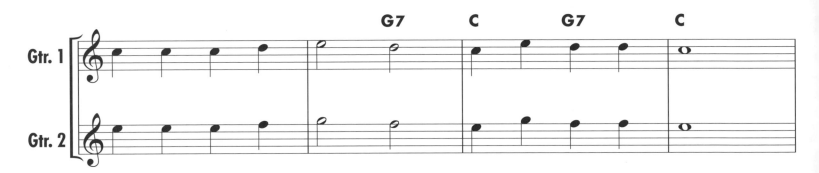

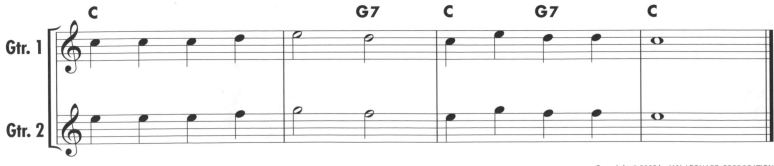

★ Regular practice on your guitar is an essential element in becoming a good player. Practicing a half hour each day is better than practicing two hours every four days. Find a regular time of the day that works for you.

PLAYING SINGLE NOTES

This next tune is a popular single-note melody using many of the notes you have learned so far. Focus on using the correct left-hand fingers for each note. When playing open-string notes, you're allowed extra time to position your left hand for the next fretted note.

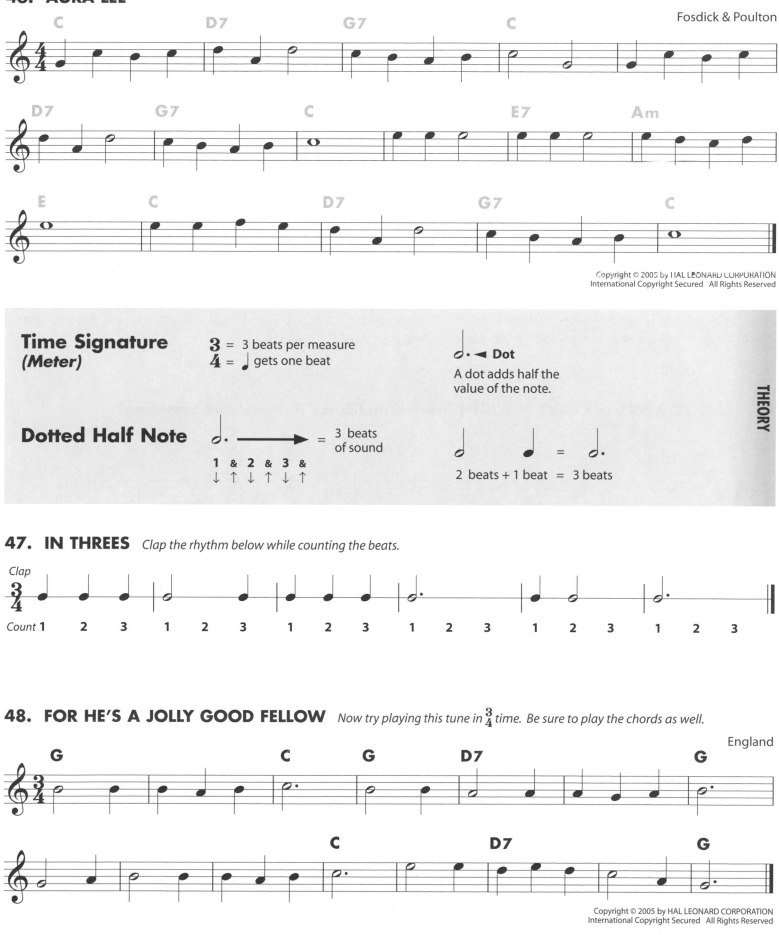

46. AURA LEE

Fosdick & Poulton

Time Signature *(Meter)*

$\frac{3}{4}$ = 3 beats per measure

= ♩ gets one beat

Dot

A dot adds half the value of the note.

Dotted Half Note = 3 beats of sound

2 beats + 1 beat = 3 beats

THEORY

47. IN THREES *Clap the rhythm below while counting the beats.*

Clap

Count 1 2 3 1 2 3 1 2 3 1 2 3 1 2 3 1 2 3

48. FOR HE'S A JOLLY GOOD FELLOW *Now try playing this tune in $\frac{3}{4}$ time. Be sure to play the chords as well.*

England

PERFORMANCE SPOTLIGHT

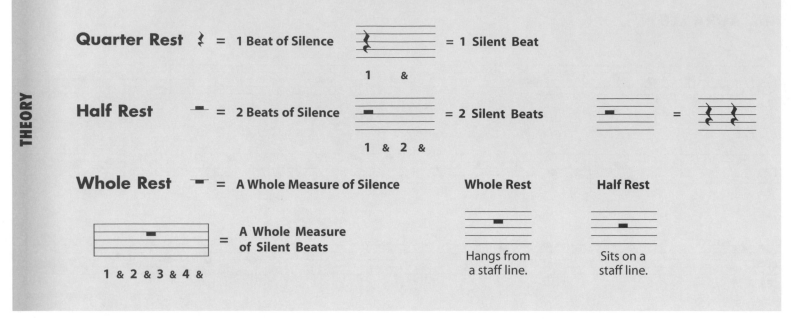

Rests   Just as there are notes of different values that tell us to play for a certain amount of time, there are **rests** of the same values that tell us *not* to play for a certain amount of time.

Quarter Rest = 1 Beat of Silence   = 1 Silent Beat

1 &

Half Rest = 2 Beats of Silence   = 2 Silent Beats

1 & 2 &

Whole Rest = A Whole Measure of Silence

= A Whole Measure of Silent Beats

1 & 2 & 3 & 4 &

Whole Rest — Hangs from a staff line.

Half Rest — Sits on a staff line.

This next song features all of the notes you have learned so far from strings 1, 2, and 3. The song splits into a duet on the next page. Be sure to observe the rests and count through them so you can keep your place in the song.

49. CAN YOU FEEL THE LOVE TONIGHT (from Walt Disney Pictures' *The Lion King*)

Verse   Elton John & Tim Rice

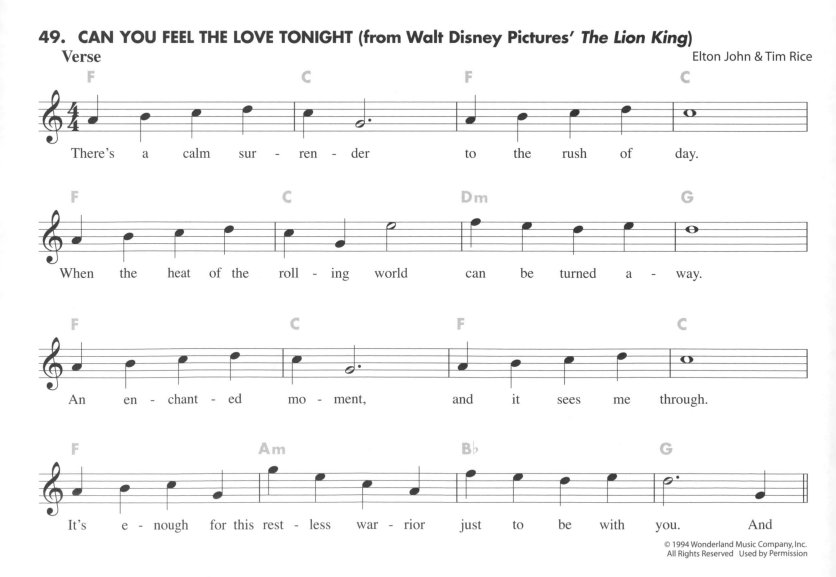

There's a calm sur - ren - der to the rush of day.

When the heat of the roll - ing world can be turned a - way.

An en - chant - ed mo - ment, and it sees me through.

It's e - nough for this rest - less war - rior just to be with you. And

PLAYING CHORDS

STRUM BUILDER 5

Syncopation   An off-beat rhythm, or the accenting of notes that fall on the "&" between counts.

Syncopated Strum

Practice the syncopated strum patterns below as a variation on the down-up stroke.

Tips
- Establish the down-up stroke pattern until you can do it without thinking.
- Continue this down-up action throughout the syncopated strum patterns, but "miss" the strings where you see the word "miss." Be sure to keep your arm moving just like the basic down-up strum.
- This will result in the desired rhythms and will allow you to easily shift back and forth from one strum pattern to another.

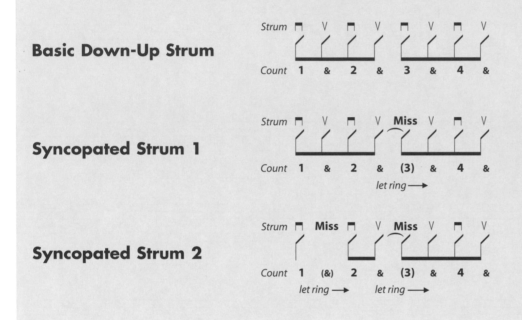

Basic Down-Up Strum

Syncopated Strum 1

Syncopated Strum 2

Try out the new strum patterns with the songs "Water Come A Me Eye" (page 7), "Pay Me My Money Down" (page 11), and "Jambalaya" (page 12), then practice them in the exercises below.

50. SYNCO DE MAYO

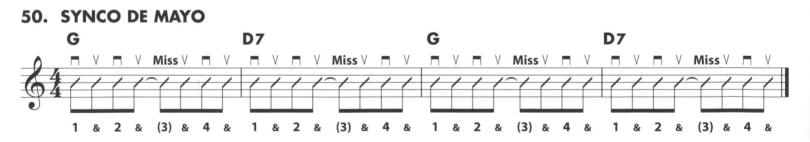

Now practice syncopated strums with the chords from "Duke of Earl."

51. DUKE OF STRUMS

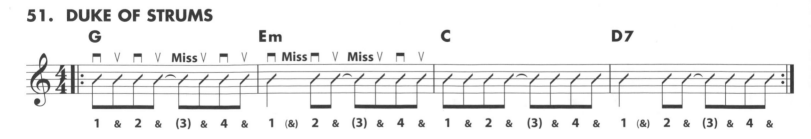

HISTORY

The syncopated strums so vital to popular music today are a result of the unique blend of African rhythms and European and Latin American musical elements.

PERFORMANCE SPOTLIGHT

Here is the full version of the song, which is a great one to try with different strum patterns. Try following the down-up strokes shown in the first line of the song. When you reach the second line, use some of the syncopated strums you've just learned.

52. DUKE OF EARL

Earl, Eugene & Bernie

53. ESSENTIAL CREATIVITY

Create your own strum patterns and play them along with the song "Duke of Earl" above. Try different combinations of the syncopated strum, the down-up strum, and the basic downstroke, or try your own original rhythms. The possibilities are limitless!

NOTES ON THE FOURTH STRING

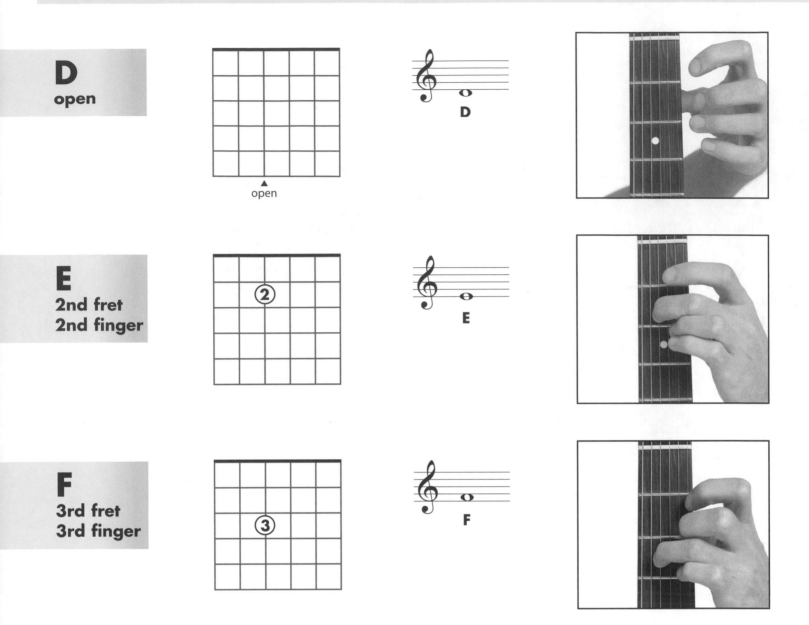

Practice each exercise carefully. Remember to keep your fingers arched over the strings.

54. FOURTH STRING WARM-UP

Hold down 2nd finger _ ꟾ

55. THE FOUR HORSEMEN

56. ESSENTIAL ELEMENTS QUIZ   *Write in the note names under the staff.*

PLAYING SINGLE NOTES

 **Alert** The next two pages include pick-up notes (see page 15). Count the missing beats out loud before you begin playing. Remember, the last measures will be short the exact number of beats as were used as pick-ups.

In the two exercises below, the final measures of each contain stacked notes. These notes should be played, or strummed, together as a chord. Notice that these chords are in fact the 3-note versions of the chords G and C which you learned earlier in the book. When you can play the melodies to these two songs, play the chord accompaniment, too.

57. THE RIDDLE SONG

Traditional

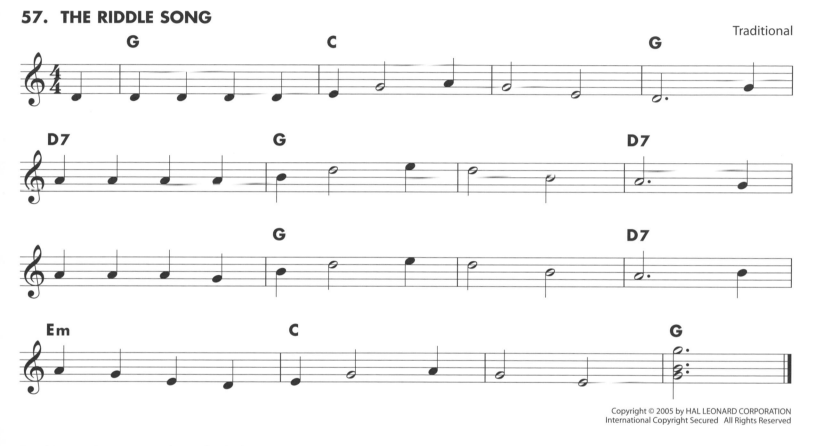

For this exercise, practice playing both the notes and then the chord strums as a duet with your teacher, a friend, or a recording device.

58. COMP-ALONG CASSIDY

59. ESSENTIAL ELEMENTS QUIZ   *Name the chords that these stacked notes create.*

PLAYING SINGLE NOTES

Try trading off playing the melodies and strumming the chords of these two songs with your teacher or friend.

60. WORRIED MAN BLUES

Traditional

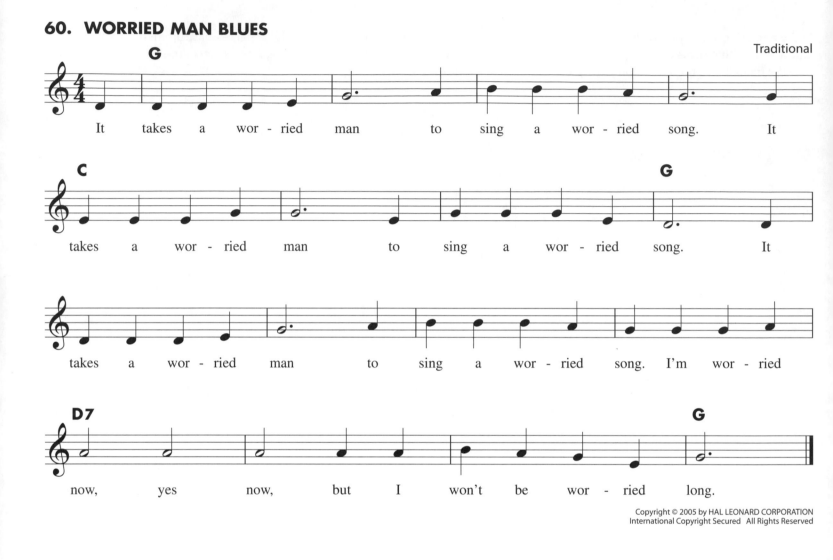

It takes a wor-ried man to sing a wor-ried song. It

takes a wor-ried man to sing a wor-ried song. It

takes a wor-ried man to sing a wor-ried song. I'm wor-ried

now, yes now, but I won't be wor-ried long.

61. 12-BAR ROCK

PERFORMANCE SPOTLIGHT

Play the melody to this famous Beatles tune while your teacher plays the chords. Be sure to sing the melody as well.

62. LET IT BE

John Lennon & Paul McCartney

PERFORMANCE SPOTLIGHT

1st and 2nd Endings

Play the 1st ending the 1st time through. Then, repeat the same section of music, skip the 1st ending, and play the 2nd ending, continuing on to the end of the song.

Try mixing different strum patterns as you play through this song. Once you can play the chord changes smoothly, try strumming *and* singing.

63. TEACH YOUR CHILDREN

Graham Nash

Intro

Verse

1. You, who are on the road—— must have a code—
(2.) you of the ten - der years—— can't know—— the

—— that you can live by. And
fears that your el - ders grew by. And so, please——

so, be - come—— your - self be - cause—— the past——
—— help them with—— your——— youth. They seek——— the

—— is just a good - bye.
truth be - fore—— they can—— die.

Chorus

Teach your chil - dren well. Their fa - ther's
Teach your par - ents well. The chil - dren's

Crosby, Stills, Nash, and Young recorded the song "Teach Your Children" in 1970. The hit song features a sweet blend of acoustic folk and country styles along with rich vocal harmonies.

HISTORY

PLAYING SINGLE NOTES

Tie

A curved line that connects two (or more) notes of the *same* pitch. The first note is struck and held for the value of both notes. The second note should not be played again. Play a single sound for the combined counts of the tied notes.

Look at the following example of tied notes. First clap the rhythms and count out loud. Then play the example while counting.

64. TIE THIS

65. AMAZING GRACE

John Newton/Traditional

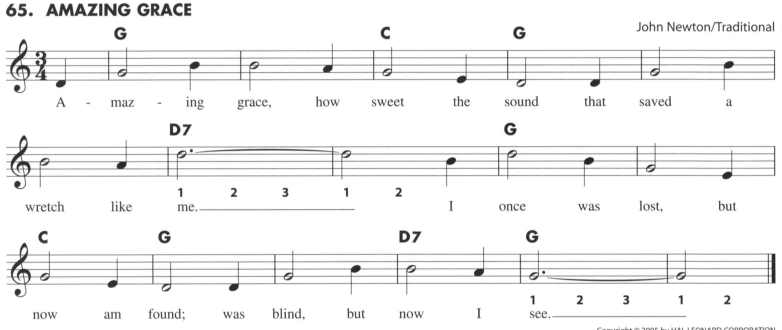

A - maz - ing grace, how sweet the sound that saved a wretch like me. I once was lost, but now am found; was blind, but now I see.

66. RIFFIN'

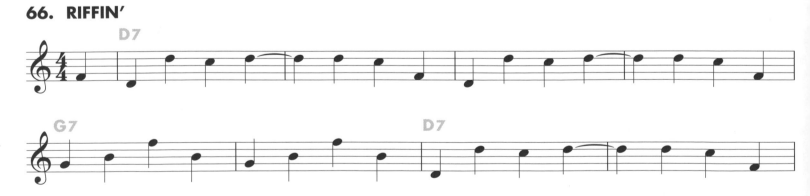

PERFORMANCE SPOTLIGHT

Practice playing both melody and chords in the following two songs. Try singing and strumming them as well.

67. WHEN THE SAINTS GO MARCHING IN

Katherine Purvis & James Black

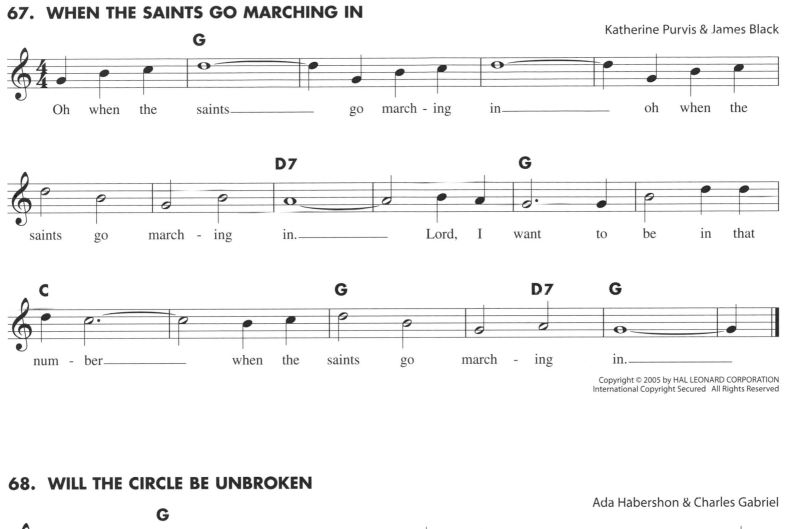

68. WILL THE CIRCLE BE UNBROKEN

Ada Habershon & Charles Gabriel

PLAYING CHORDS

D
Chord

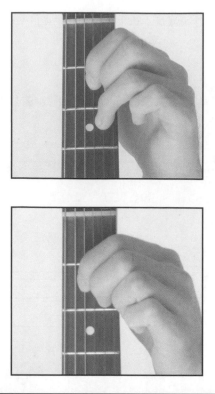

A7
Chord

STRUM BUILDER 6

Tips for Playing Chords

- Keep a steady beat with your toe or a metronome.

- When approaching a chord change, get to the new chord on time even if it means leaving the old chord a bit early.

- Try to move your fingers to a new chord as a single "unit" instead of "letting your fingers do the walking" one at a time.

Try out the new chords D and A7 in the following tune. When you have the chords down, try one of the syncopated strums.

69. MARIANNE

Caribbean

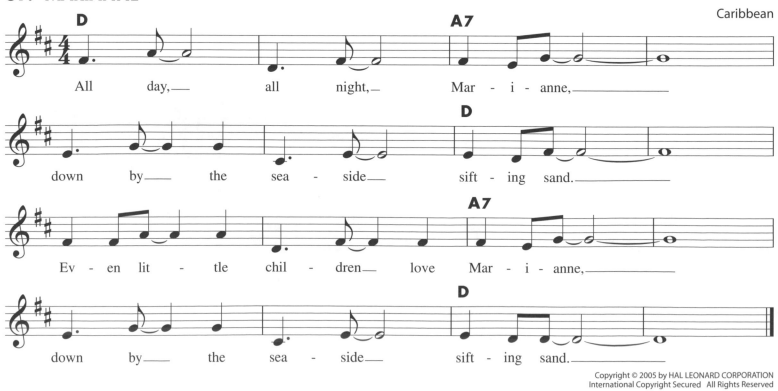

All day,— all night,— Mar - i - anne,—
down by— the sea - side— sift - ing sand.—
Ev - en lit - tle chil - dren— love Mar - i - anne,—
down by— the sea - side— sift - ing sand.—

PLAYING CHORDS

Strum and sing this African-American traditional tune that features the new chords D and A7. Play the repeats until you've sung all the verses.

70. THIS TRAIN

71. ESSENTIAL ELEMENTS QUIZ *Write in the number of beats that the tied notes last.*

PLAYING CHORDS

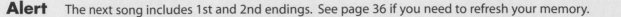

🎵 **Alert** The next song includes 1st and 2nd endings. See page 36 if you need to refresh your memory.

72. SURFIN' U.S.A. *Strum and sing this famous Beach Boys song.*

Chuck Berry

Ev - 'ry - bod - y's gone surf - in',_____ surf - in' U. S. A._____

____ 1. If ev - 'ry - bod - y had an o - cean_____ a - cross the U. S. A._____
(2.) route_____ we're gon - na take real soon..

_____ Then ev - 'ry - bod - y'd be surf - in'_____
_____ We're wax - in' down____ our surf - boards_____

____ like Cal - i - for - ni - a._____ You'd see them wear - in' their
____ we can't____ wait for June._____ We'll all be gone for the

bag - gies,_____ huar - a - chi san - dals too._____
sum - mer,_____ we're on sa - fa - ri to stay._____

____ A bush - y, bush - y blonde hair - do,_____ surf - in' U. S. A._____
Tell the teach - er we're surf - in',_____ surf - in' U. S. A._____

You'll catch 'em surf - in' at Del Mar,_____
At Hag - gar - ty's_____ and Swam - i's,_____

___ Ven - tu - ra Coun - ty Line._____ San - ta Cruz and
___ Pac - if - ic Pal - i - sades._____ San O - nofre and

Tress - els,_____ ___ Aus - tra - lia's Nar - a - bine._____
Sun - set_____ Re - don - do Beach, L. A._____

___ All o - ver Man - hat - tan,_____ and down Do - he - ny way.___
___ All o - ver La Jol - la,_____ at Wai - a - me - a Bay.__

Ev - 'ry - bod - y's gone surf - in',_____
Ev - 'ry - body's gone gone surf - in',_____

1.
___ surf - in' U. S. A._____ 2. We'll all be plan - nin' out a ___
___ surf - in' U. S. A._____

The Beach Boys helped popularize the surf guitar music craze of the 1960s with such hits as "Surfin' U.S.A.," "Good Vibrations," "I Get Around," "Fun, Fun, Fun," and many more. They were perhaps best known for their signature use of catchy vocal harmony lines.

HISTORY

PLAYING CHORDS

STRUM BUILDER 7

Bass/Strum Technique

A right-hand strumming technique that involves first playing the single bass note of a chord followed by a strum of the rest of the chord.

Bass/Strum Methods

- With a **pick**: Play a single bass string, then strum lightly downward across the remaining treble strings.

- With the **thumb**: Pluck a single bass string with the thumb, then strum downward across the remaining treble strings with the fleshy part of the thumb.

- With the **thumb and fingers**: Pluck a single bass note with the thumb, then strum downward across the treble strings with the fingernail of the index (and middle) fingers.

Bass/Strum Patterns

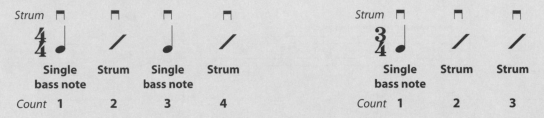

Playing the proper bass string for each chord will take some practice. Below is a chart showing the correct bass string number for each of the chords you know.

Chords:	A7	C	D or D7	Em	G or G7
Bass String:	5	5	4	6	6

Practice the following bass/strum exercises which indicate the string number for each single bass note and a slash mark for the strum. When you can play these patterns with ease, go back to the songs "Marianne" (page 40) and "This Train" (page 41) and apply the bass/strum technique.

73. BASS/STRUM WORKOUT

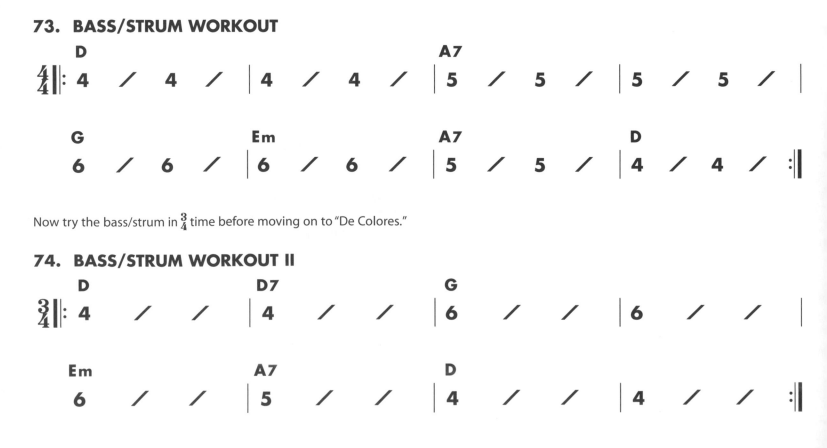

Now try the bass/strum in ¾ time before moving on to "De Colores."

74. BASS/STRUM WORKOUT II

PLAYING CHORDS

75. DE COLORES *Play the accompaniment to this tune using the bass/strum 3/4 pattern. You can sing the melody, too.*

Mexican Folk Song

All _____ the col - ors, all the col - ors that bloom in the
De _____ co - lo - res, de co - lo - res se vis - ten los

mead - ows are col - ors of spring - time. _____
cam - pos en la pri - ma - ve - ra. _____

All _____ the col - ors, all the col - ors that dance in the
De _____ co - lo - res, de co - lo - res son los pa - ja -

sky are the col - ors of rain - bows. _____
ri - tos que vie - nen de a fue - ra. _____

All _____ the col - ors, all the col - ors of na - ture spring
De _____ co - lo - res, de co - lo - res es el ar - co

forth _____ to make my heart sing. Then I know why the col - ors of
i - ris _____ que ve - mos lu - cir, y por e - so los gran - des a -

spring - time are bring - ing me joy and _____ a heart full of love.
mo - res de mu - chos co - lo - res _____ me gus - tan a mí.

NOTES ON THE FIFTH STRING

THEORY

Ledger Line 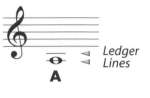 Extends the range of the music staff. Notes on **ledger lines** can be above or below the staff.

A
open

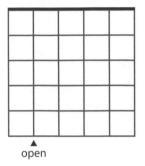

open

Ledger Lines

A

B
2nd fret
2nd finger

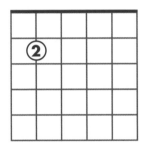

B

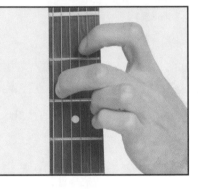

C
3rd fret
3rd finger

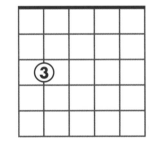

C

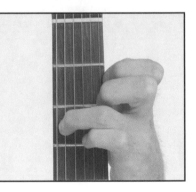

Play through the following exercises that use notes on the fifth string.

76. FIFTH STRING WARM-UP

Hold down 2nd finger – ⌐

77. BLUES BASS

A   D7

A   E7   D7   A

PLAYING SINGLE NOTES

Practice these familiar melodies until you feel comfortable playing them. Remember to look ahead as you play so you can prepare for the next notes.

78. JOSHUA (FIT THE BATTLE OF JERICHO)

African-American Spiritual

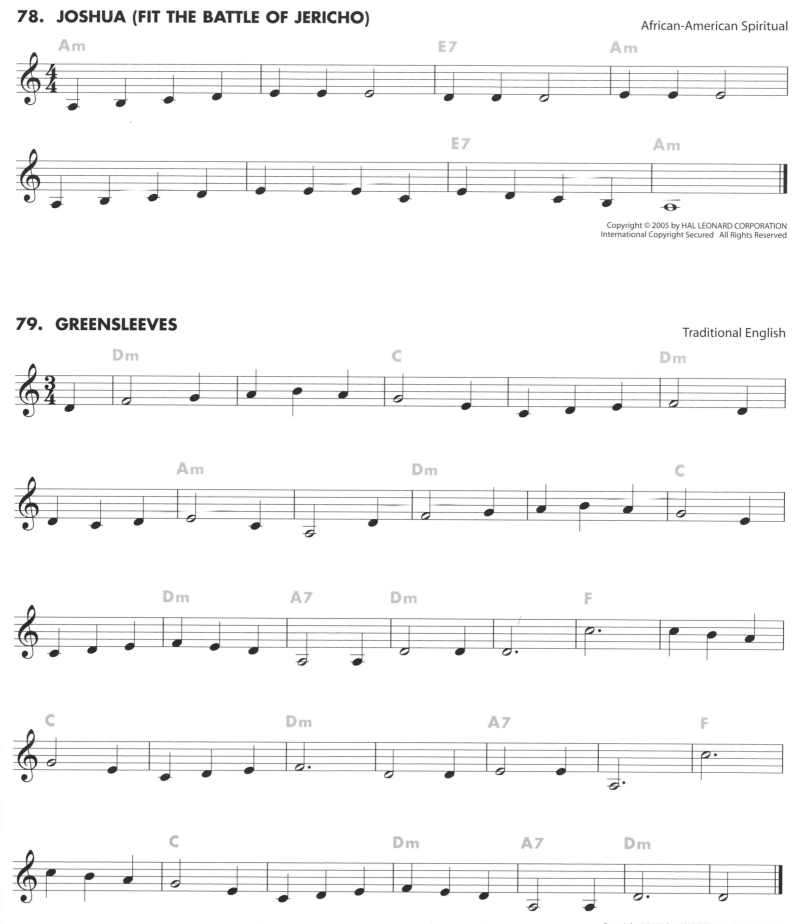

79. GREENSLEEVES

Traditional English

PLAYING CHORDS

Study the diagram below to play the Em7 chord. Another version can also be played. See the Chord Chart on page 94 to learn the alternate Em7 chord.

Em7
Chord

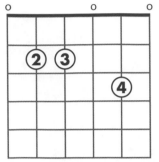

Try out the Em7 chord as you practice the tune below. Also you should experiment with various strum patterns such as the syncopated strums (page 30). This is a fun song to sing while you play. Play the alternate (Am) chords after you have learned them on page 51.

80. AMERICAN PIE

D7   **Em**   **D7**   **C**

love with him— 'cause I   saw you danc-in' in the gym.— You both kicked off— your
look-ing down,— the   jest-er stole his thorn-y crown. The court-room was ad-journed.—

A7   **C**   **D7**   **G**   **D**

shoes.— Man, I   dig those rhy-thm and blues.— I was a lone-ly teen-age—
— No— ver-dict was re-turned.— And while Len-in read a book—

Em7   **C (Am)**   **C**   **G**   **D**

bronc-in' buck— with a pink car-na-tion and a pick-up truck.— But I knew I— was
— on— Marx,— a quar-tet prac-ticed in the park.— And we sang dir-ges

Em7   **C**   **D7**   **G** **C**   **1.** **G**   **D7**   **2.** **G** **D7** **G**

out— of luck— the day the mu-sic died.   I start-ed sing-in'
— in the dark, the day the mu-sic died.

PLAYING SINGLE NOTES

Your teacher will play the chords as you pick out the melody to this Hank Williams classic. After you can play the melody, try singing along.

81. YOUR CHEATIN' HEART

Hank Williams

Verse   **C**   **C7**   **F**   **G7**

Your cheat-in' heart— will make you weep.— You'll cry and cry,— and try to

C   **G7**   **C**   **C7**   **F**

sleep.— But sleep won't come— the whole night through;— your cheat-in'

G7   **C**   **C7**   **F**   **Bridge**

heart— will tell on you.— When tears come down— like fall-in'

C   **D7**   **G7**

rain,— you'll toss a-round— and call my name.— You'll walk the

Chorus   **C**   **C7**   **F**   **G7**   **C**

floor— the way I do;— your cheat-in' heart— will tell on you.—

PERFORMANCE SPOTLIGHT

Practice both parts of the following duet. Ask a classmate to play the duet along with you.

82. ALL MY LOVING

John Lennon & Paul McCartney

⭐ Remember to have fun as you practice your instrument. Don't be afraid to try different things; experiment, explore, and create your own music.

PLAYING CHORDS

The bass string for the new chord Am is string 5.

 Am Chord

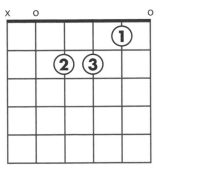

Practice changing chords in the following examples. Play slowly and steadily so there is no hesitation between chords.

83. STRIKE A CHORD

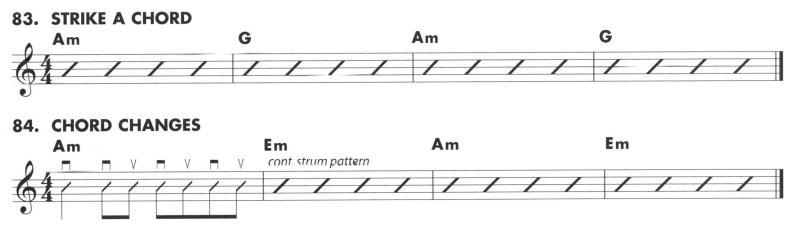

84. CHORD CHANGES

85. SINNER MAN *Play the chords and sing along.*

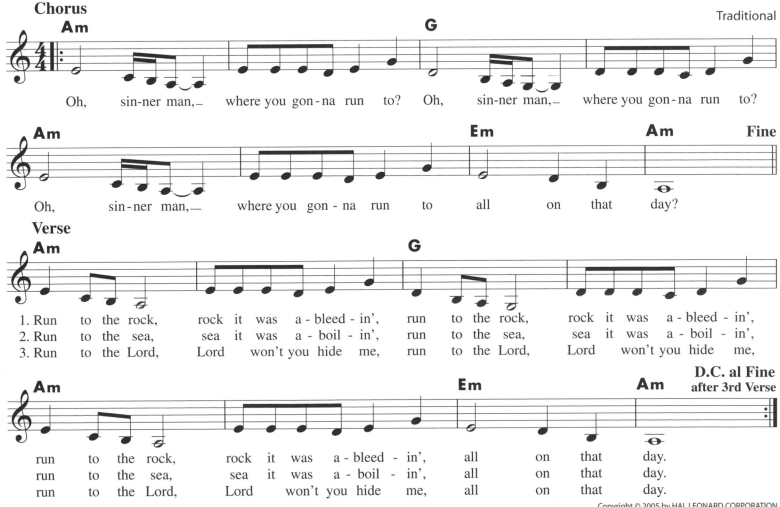

NOTES ON THE SIXTH STRING

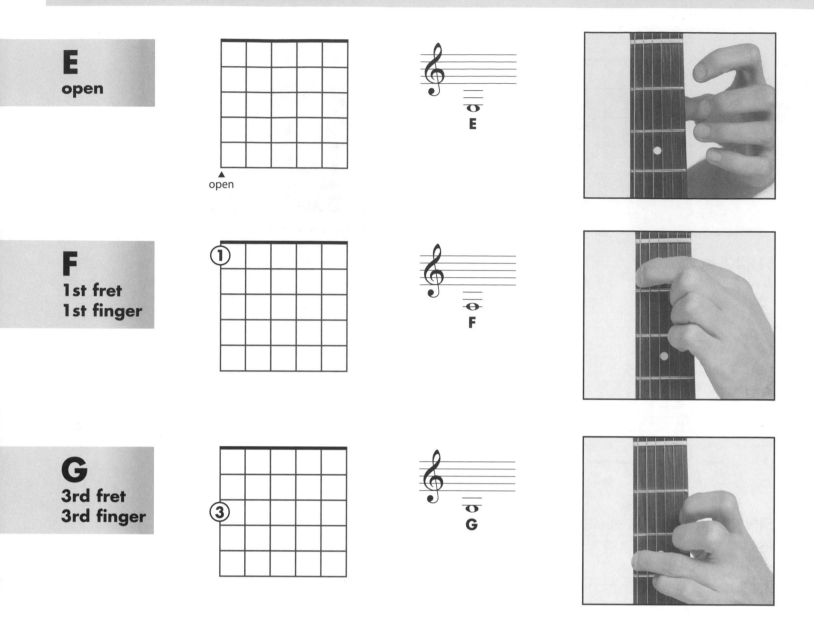

E
open

F
1st fret
1st finger

G
3rd fret
3rd finger

Play through the following exercises that include notes on the sixth string.

86. SIXTH STRING WARM-UP

Hold down 1st finger - - - - - - - - - - - - - - - - - - - |

87. STRING 'EM UP

88. THE LOW DOWN

PLAYING SINGLE NOTES

Play through these tunes that include notes from strings 4 through 6. Remember to arch your hand so you don't touch any of the other strings as you play.

89. DOO-WOP

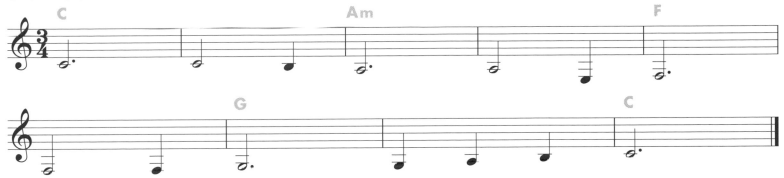

90. GIVE MY REGARDS TO BROADWAY

George M. Cohan

91. BASS ROCK

PLAYING CHORDS

The Am7 chord is a variation of the Am chord. Simply subtract your 3rd finger and play the third string (G) open instead. Be sure to arch your fingers enough to allow string 3 to ring. Also be careful not to mix up this chord with A7. The bass string for Am7 is string 5.

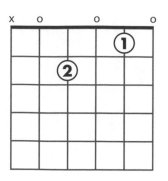

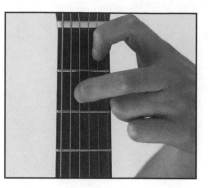

Practice the Am7 chord by playing the following exercises. Try using the bass/strum technique on these exercises as well.

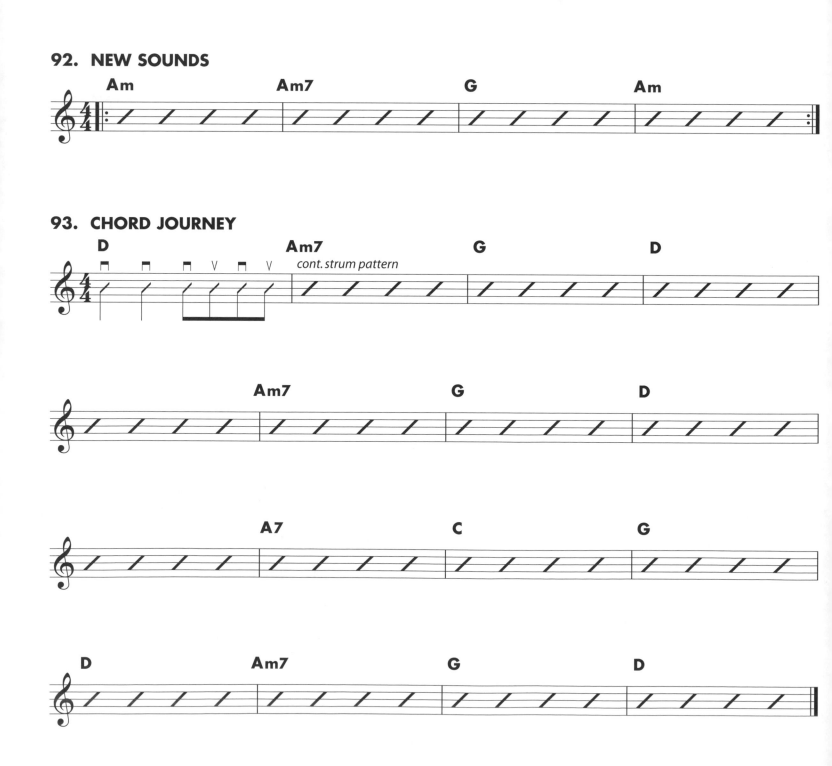

PLAYING CHORDS

94. SCARBOROUGH FAIR

Traditional English

The traditional song "Scarborough Fair" was composed hundreds of years ago in the country of England. In the Middle Ages, songs were often performed by *bards* or *traveling minstrels* who made a living by going from town to town singing songs and telling stories. When these songs were heard and spread to various towns, the lyrics and arrangements would change, resulting in many different versions. In turn, these different versions were passed down through generations by way of *oral tradition*. This is why today there are many versions of "Scarborough Fair" being performed by many different artists. Perhaps the most well-known version was recorded by Simon & Garfunkel in 1966.

HISTORY

FINGER PICKING

Arpeggio	An **arpeggio** is a "broken" chord whose notes are played individually and in succession instead of all at the same time.
Finger Picking	A very popular style of guitar accompaniment which uses arpeggios instead of strummed chords. The distinctive sound of **finger picking** comes from the right-hand thumb and fingers plucking only one string each in succession.

The Right Hand

The right-hand thumb and fingers are given letters based on the internationally accepted system of Spanish words and letters:

p = **pulgar** = thumb

i   = **indice** = index finger

m = **medio** = middle finger

a   = **anular** = ring finger

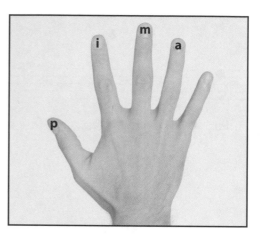

Right-Hand Technique

- The thumb (p) plucks strings 4, 5, or 6 depending upon which string has the bass note of the chord. This motion is a downward stroke. Use the left side of the thumb and thumbnail.

- The other fingers (i, m, a) pluck the string in an upward stroke with the fleshy tip of the finger and fingernail.

- The index finger (i) plucks string 3.

- The middle finger (m) plucks string 2.

- The ring finger (a) plucks string 1.

- The thumb and each finger must pluck only one string per stroke and not brush over several strings (this would be a strum). Let the strings ring throughout the duration of the chord.

Right-Hand Position

- Use a high wrist and position your thumb and fingers over their respective strings.

- Arch your palm as if you were holding a ping-pong ball.

- Keep your thumb and fingers relaxed and ready to play.

- Let the fingers do the work rather than lifting your whole hand.

FINGER PICKING

The following exercise uses a staff with six lines to represent each string of the guitar. Practice the finger-picking patterns as indicated by the p–i–m–a letters. Remember that the thumb (p) plucks the bass note of each chord. This six-lined staff is similar to *tablature*, which you will learn about later in the book.

95. FINGER-PICKIN' GOOD

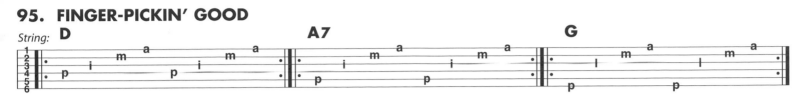

Now use the p–i–m–a pattern of finger picking you have just learned as an accompaniment to the next tune. The finger-picking staff is given below the first line of music to help you see the relationship of one pluck per beat. See the additional words following the song to sing the verses.

96. WORRIED MAN BLUES

1. Twenty-nine links of chain around my leg, *(3 times)*
   And on each link an initial of my name.
   To Chorus

2. I asked the judge, "What might be my fine?" *(3 times)*
   "Twenty-one years on the Rocky Mountain Line."
   To Chorus

3. If anyone should ask you "Who made up this song?" *(3 times)*
   Say, "'Twas I, and I sing it all night long."
   To Chorus

NEW NOTES

Some songs require you to learn a new note or technique in order to perform them. Often just one or two additional skills are needed to perform a new song. Here is an example of that. The new notes A and B above the staff can be played with the fourth finger (pinky) on the first string. This requires you to slide your hand position on the fretboard up a few frets so that your pinky can reach frets 5 and 7.

A
5th fret
4th finger

B
7th fret
4th finger

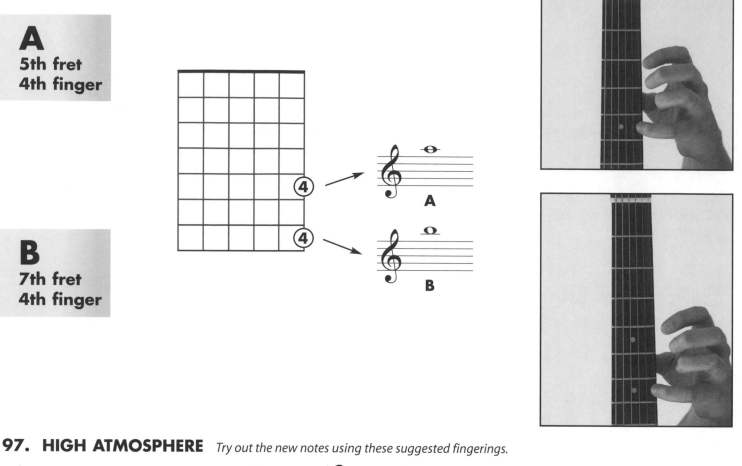

97. HIGH ATMOSPHERE *Try out the new notes using these suggested fingerings.*

The new notes A and B above the staff can be played with fingers other than the fourth finger depending upon where your left-hand position is on the fretboard. Different songs will require different positions, and likewise fingerings (for other notes, too), as shown by the excerpt from the song "Danny Boy" below. Practice this new fingering before you play the full version on the next page.

98. DAN

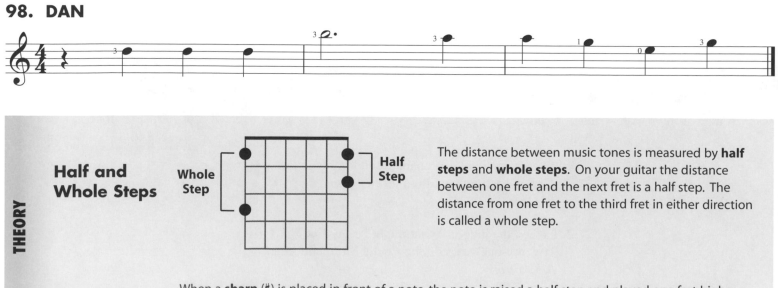

THEORY

Half and Whole Steps

Whole Step

Half Step

The distance between music tones is measured by **half steps** and **whole steps**. On your guitar the distance between one fret and the next fret is a half step. The distance from one fret to the third fret in either direction is called a whole step.

Sharp ♯

When a **sharp** (♯) is placed in front of a note, the note is raised a half step and played one fret higher. A sharp placed before a note affects all notes on the same line or space that follow in that measure.

NEW NOTES

Below are three different F# notes on the fretboard to learn and play. Just move up one fret (or half step) from any of the regular F notes that you already know.

3 F#s

F#

99. THE F-SHARPS *Practice each of these finger exercises many times.*

Now play both parts of "Danny Boy" which use all of the new notes. Play as a duet with your friend or teacher. Also you can play the chord progression as a third part.

Weatherly/Traditional Irish

100. DANNY BOY

Oh, Dan-ny boy, the pipes, the pipes are call-ing,—— from glen to glen, and down the moun-tain side.—— The sum-mer's gone, and all the ros-es fall-ing.—— It's you, it's you must go and I must bide.—— But come ye back when sum-mer's in the mead-ow,—— or when the val-ley's hushed and white with snow.—— Tis I'll be there in sun-shine or in shad-ow.—— Oh, Dan-ny boy, oh Dan-ny boy, I love you so!

PERFORMANCE SPOTLIGHT

THEORY

Key Signature

Instead of writing a sharp sign (#) before every F in a song, one sharp is placed at the beginning of the line. This is called a **key signature** and indicates that every F in the song should be played as F#.

Play through the following songs that include key signatures. Notice that the tunes on this page include arrows on each F# as a reminder. After you can play the melody with the F#'s successfully, add in the chord progression with a friend.

101. SHENANDOAH

American Folksong

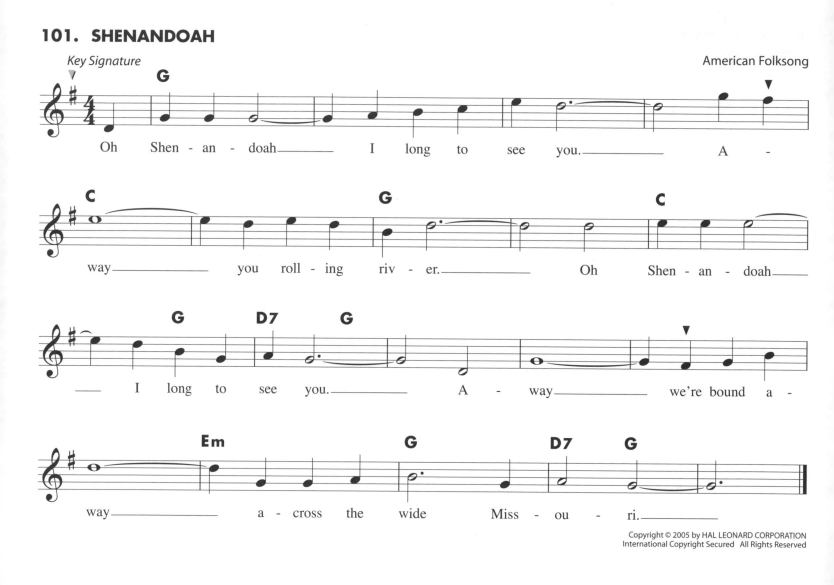

Oh Shen - an - doah I long to see you. A -
way you roll - ing riv - er. Oh Shen - an - doah
I long to see you. A - way we're bound a -
way a - cross the wide Miss - ou - ri.

102. SPY RIFF

PERFORMANCE SPOTLIGHT

After you're able to play through the melodies of the next two songs, sing and strum the tunes as well. Then try out the finger-picking and bass/strum techniques. The bass string for the C chord is string 5.

103. THE RED RIVER VALLEY

American Cowboy Song

104. CORINNA

Traditional

PLAYING CHORDS

The A chord is a lot like the A7 chord with the "space" (third string) filled in. Arch your fingers so the first string rings as an open string. The open fifth string (A) is the bass note for the A chord.

A
Chord

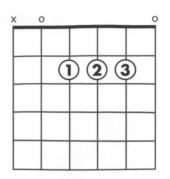

STRUM BUILDER 8

Down/Up Stroke Variation

Practice the new strum pattern below as a variation on the basic down/up stroke.

Tips

- Instead of using an even down/up stroke rhythm as you have been, use an uneven rhythmic approach, or "gallop."
- Make the downstroke last longer than the upstroke.
- Say "bump-ty, bump-ty, bump-ty, bump-ty" as you try the strum variation to help yourself feel the rhythm.
- This same rhythm is sometimes called a "dotted" rhythm because it uses dotted notes. This is also similar to a "shuffle" feel, which we will explore later in the book.

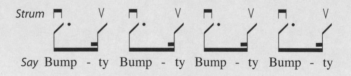

Practice the new strum variation in the exercise below which includes the chord changes from "Yellow Submarine" before moving on to the actual song.

105. HUMPTY BUMPTY

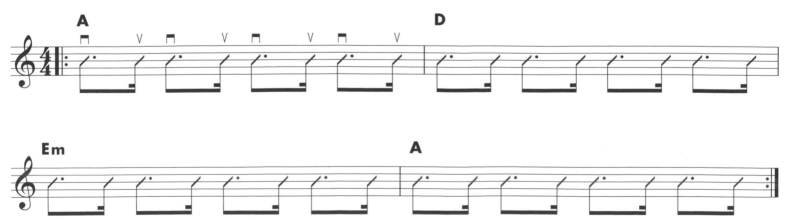

PLAYING CHORDS

Play the chords to this song using the new down/up stroke variation. Then try playing with the bass/strum and finger-picking techniques.

106. YELLOW SUBMARINE

John Lennon & Paul McCartney

PLAYING CHORDS

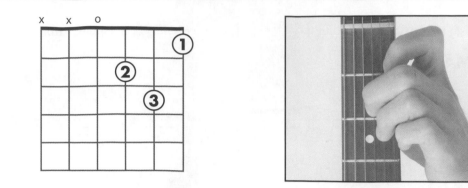

Dm
Chord

Practice changing chords with Dm in the following exercise before moving on to the next song. The bass string for Dm is string 4.

107. MINOR CHORD PRACTICE

108. WAYFARING STRANGER
After you've played the chords, learn the melody as well; then try the bass/strum and finger-picking techniques.

American Folk Hymn

PLAYING SINGLE NOTES

Eighth Notes

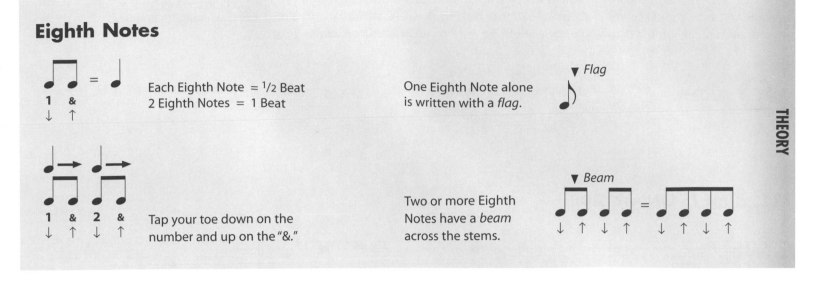

Each Eighth Note = 1/2 Beat
2 Eighth Notes = 1 Beat

One Eighth Note alone is written with a *flag*.

Tap your toe down on the number and up on the "&."

Two or more Eighth Notes have a *beam* across the stems.

Alternate Picking

Eighth notes are played with a downstroke (⊓) of the pick on the beat and an upstroke (V) on the "and." This is called **alternate picking** and is basically the same technique as the down/up stroke for chord strumming, but here is used for single-note picking.

Play the following exercises using alternate picking for all eighth notes and strictly downstrokes for all quarter notes. Practice slowly and steadily at first, then gradually increase the speed.

109. EIGHTH NOTES

110. MIX IT UP

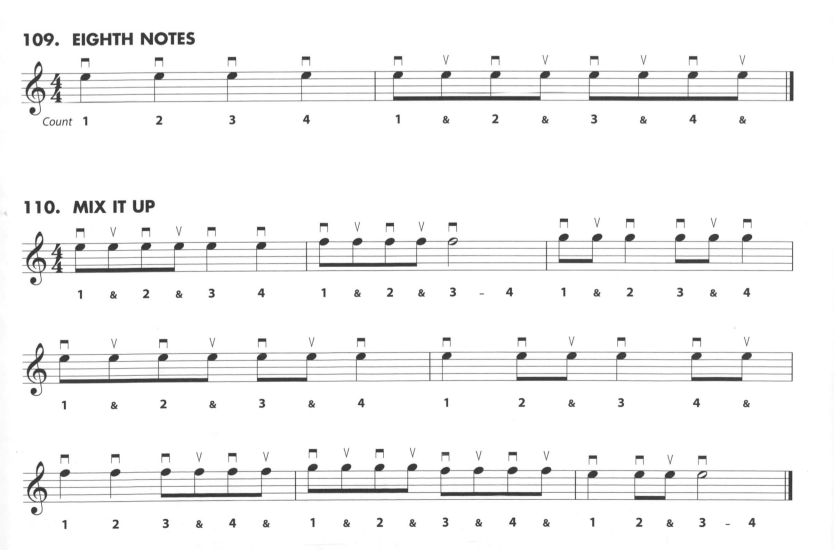

PERFORMANCE SPOTLIGHT

Get acquainted with eighth notes and alternate picking on the next several songs. When you feel comfortable playing the melodies, go back and try some chord accompaniment using finger picking, down/up stroke variations, and the bass/strum technique. Follow the finger-picking staff on "Time is on My Side" to play a finger-picking accompaniment with a 3/4 pattern.

 Alert The next song includes a key signature (with one sharp). Remember that this means all of the F notes in the song are played as F♯.

111. TIME IS ON MY SIDE

Jerry Ragovoy

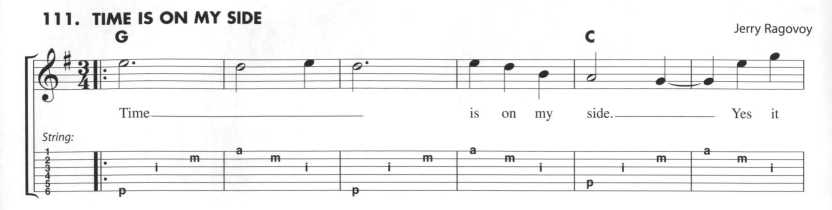

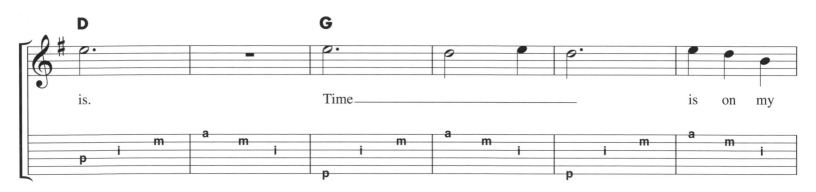

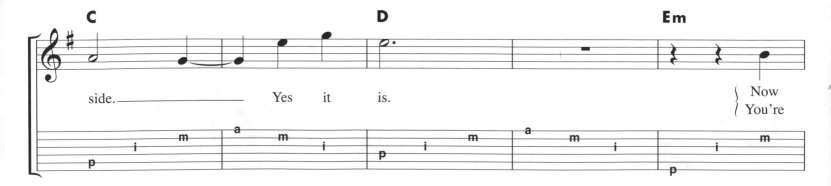

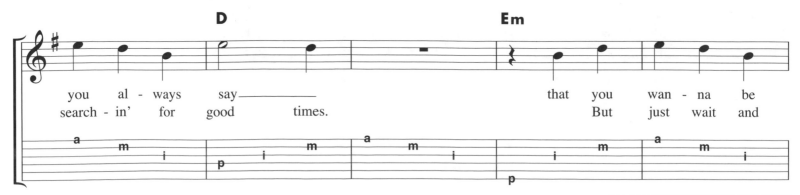

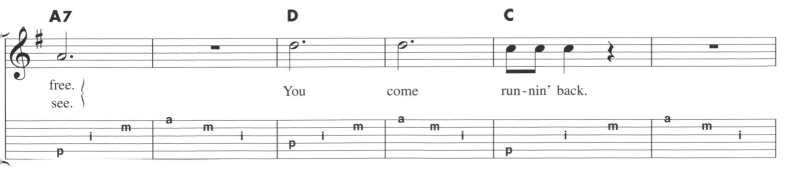

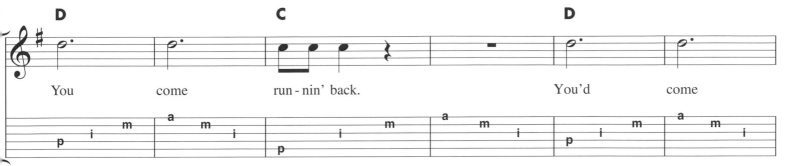

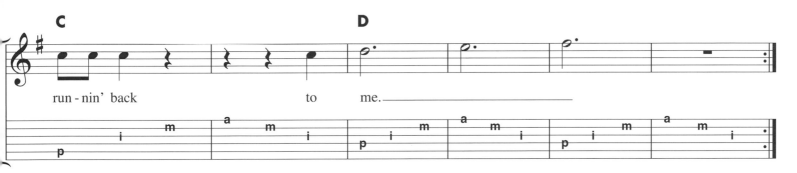

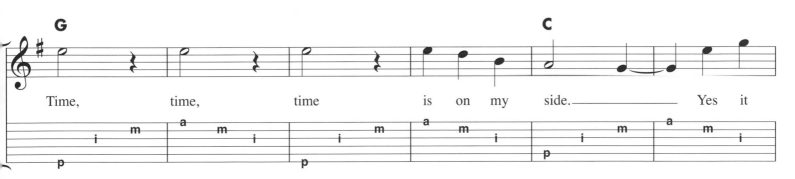

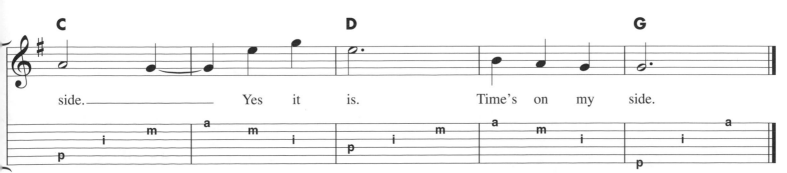

PERFORMANCE SPOTLIGHT

112. STAND BY ME

Jerry Leiber, Mike Stoller & Ben E. King

PERFORMANCE SPOTLIGHT

| **Octave** | The distance between two notes of the same letter name. |

113. SEA SHANTY

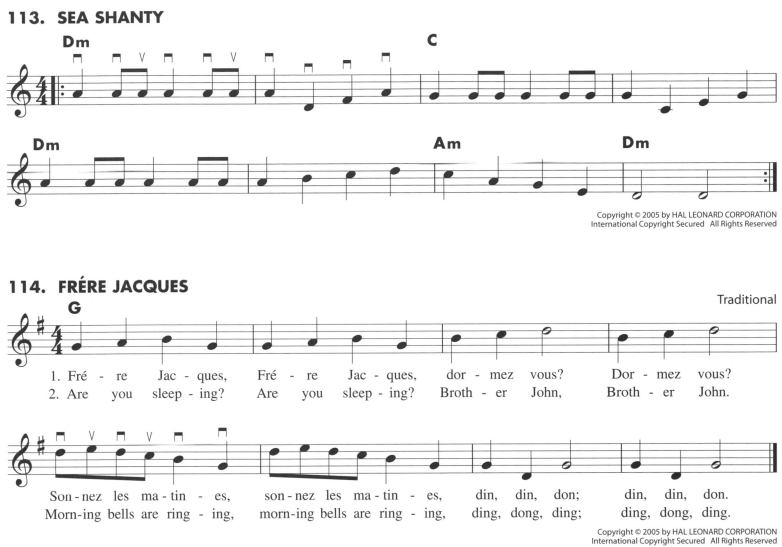

114. FRÉRE JACQUES

Traditional

1. Fré - re   Jac - ques,   Fré - re   Jac - ques,   dor - mez   vous?   Dor - mez   vous?
2. Are   you   sleep - ing?   Are   you   sleep - ing?   Broth - er   John,   Broth - er   John.

Son - nez les ma - tin - es,   son - nez les ma - tin - es,   din, din, don;   din, din, don.
Morn-ing bells are ring - ing,   morn-ing bells are ring - ing,   ding, dong, ding;   ding, dong, ding.

115. SNAKE CHARMER

Traditional

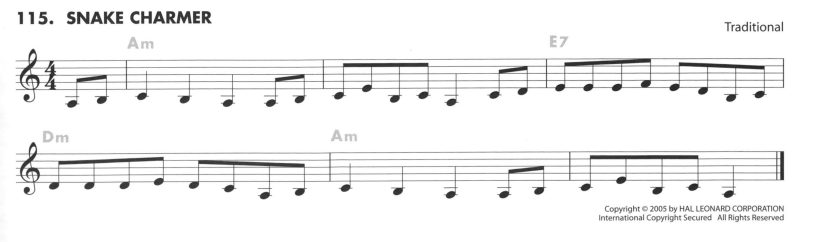

116. ESSENTIAL ELEMENTS QUIZ

Try playing "Snake Charmer" again, this time on the higher strings. Begin one octave higher with the A note on the second fret of the third string, and use your ear as a guide.

PLAYING CHORDS

The E chord is played with the same finger formation as the Am chord, except that the fingers are moved one string over to strings 3, 4, and 5. The open sixth string (E) is the bass note.

E Chord

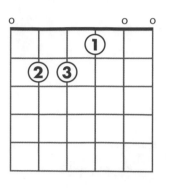

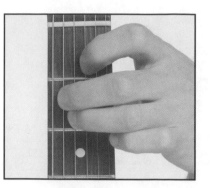

D.S. al Coda

At the **D.S. al Coda** go back to the sign 𝄋, then play through until you reach the "To Coda ⊕" sign. Next, jump to the **Coda** section at the end of the music and play to the end. **D.S.** is the abbreviation for Dal Segno, or "from the sign," and **Coda** means "tail."

Try out the new E chord while you sing along to this Beatles classic. Watch for the new musical direction, D.S. al Coda; trace the musical roadmap with your eyes first before playing. Also use the bass/strum and finger-picking techniques for accompaniment.

117. HEY JUDE

John Lennon & Paul McCartney

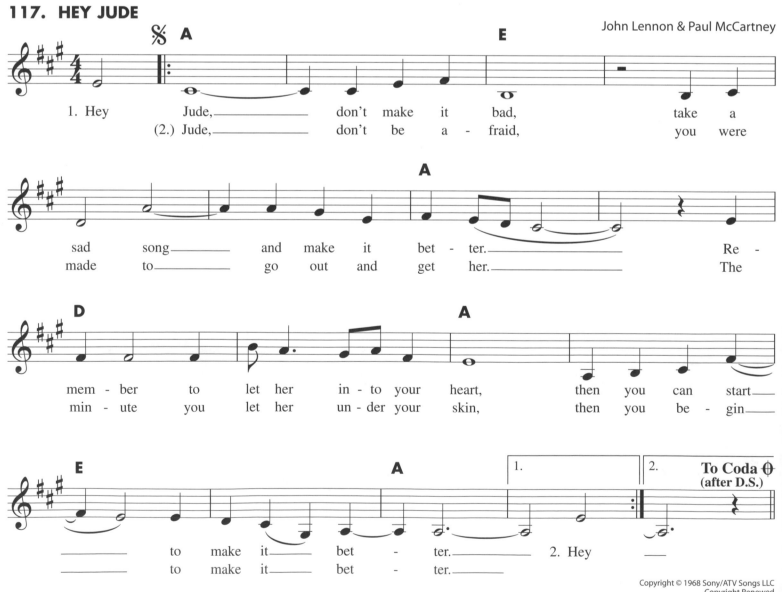

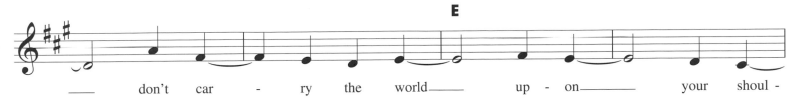

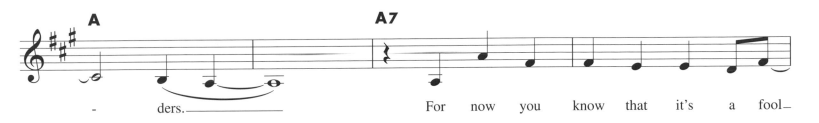

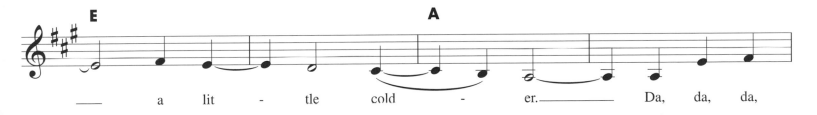

FINGER PICKING

The following tune, made popular by Kermit the Frog, is a great review of chords and finger picking. First play through the song with the bass/strum technique (notice the $\frac{3}{4}$ time signature) to practice the chord changes. Then use finger picking. Watch the first line of music for help with the finger picking sequence.

118. THE RAINBOW CONNECTION (from *The Muppet Movie*)

Paul Williams & Kenneth L. Ascher

continue finger picking throughout

Chorus

So we've been told, and some choose to be - lieve it;
What's so a - maz - ing that keeps us star gaz - ing and
I've heard it too man - y times to ig - nore it. It's

I know they're wrong; wait and see.
what do we think we and might see?
some - thing that I'm s'posed to be.

Some - day we'll find it, the rain - bow con - nec - tion; the

lov - ers, the dream-ers, and me.

Play 3 times

119. ESSENTIAL ELEMENTS QUIZ *Name the bass string number for each chord.*

G   C   D7   Am   Em   Dm   A   E   Am7

___   ___   ___   ___   ___   ___   ___   ___   ___

PERFORMANCE SPOTLIGHT

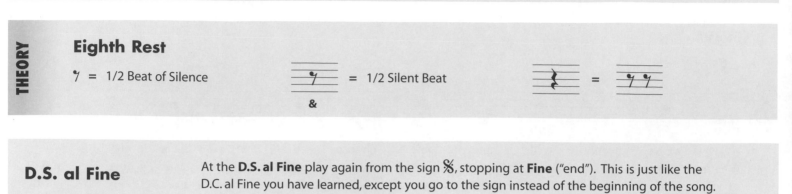

THEORY

Eighth Rest

γ = 1/2 Beat of Silence   = 1/2 Silent Beat   =

D.S. al Fine

At the **D.S. al Fine** play again from the sign 𝄋, stopping at **Fine** ("end"). This is just like the D.C. al Fine you have learned, except you go to the sign instead of the beginning of the song.

Play this next song by The Police which contains several elements that you have recently learned, including eighth rests. Try picking the melody as well as singing, strumming, and finger picking.

120. EVERY BREATH YOU TAKE

Sting

FINGER PICKING

This next song is well-known for its finger-picked guitar accompaniment. Play the melody first, and then try finger picking the chords and singing. Experiment with different finger-picking sequences.

121. DUST IN THE WIND

Kerry Livgren

PLAYING CHORDS

Power Chords

Power Chords are commonly used in rock and other contemporary music. Most chords have three or more notes, power chords have just two. Power chords are labeled with the suffix "5."

E5
Chord

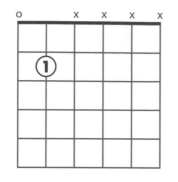

A5
Chord

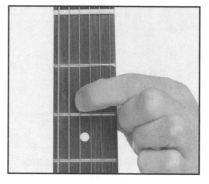

D5
Chord

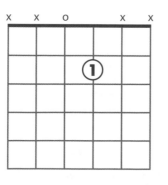

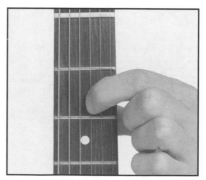

122. POWER CHORD WARM-UP

PLAYING CHORDS

STRUM BUILDER 9

The Shuffle
In traditional music styles like blues and jazz, eighth notes are played unevenly. This style of playing is known as **the shuffle** or swing feel.

Play the first note twice as long as the second note.

1 - 2   3
long   short

Playing the eighth notes in this way will give you the desired shuffle or swing feel. This concept is similar to the "dotted" rhythm strum variation (page 62).

Tablature
A graphic representation of the guitar fretboard. Each horizontal line represents a string and each number represents a fret. **Tablature** is often used along with written guitar music to help the player see more specifically where the music is to be played.

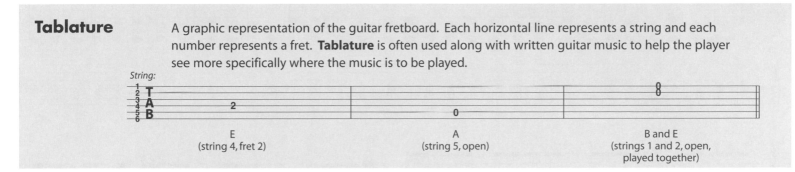

Play the tune below with a shuffle feel. Follow the accompanying tablature to play the power chords in a blues style. Notice there are certain notes that you haven't learned yet, as well as different ways to play notes that you already know. This power chord pattern involves the use of your third finger on the 4th fret on beats 2 and 4, creating a back-and-forth motion between the power chord and 4th fret fingerings. The tablature will help you to see and play the relatively simple pattern of this blues shuffle.

123. POWER CHORD SHUFFLE

PLAYING CHORDS

12-Bar Blues
The most typical blues is twelve measures, or *bars*, long.

Many 12-bar blues songs follow the chord progression in the next exercise. Use the power chord shuffle you have just learned.

124. BLUES IN A

125. C.C. RIDER
Play this 12-bar blues song with the power chord shuffle from the previous exercise and sing along; then try it with regular chords.

Traditional

1. C.   C.   rid - er,___   see   what   you   have   done.___   C.   C.   rid - er,
2. Tell   me   rid - er,___   what   is   on   your   mind.___   Tell   me   rid - er,

see what you have done.___   You made me love you,   now your friend has come.___
what is on your mind.___   Oh, tell me why you   treat me so un - kind.___

126. ESSENTIAL CREATIVITY

Now go back and play the blues song "Sweet Home Chicago" (page 16) with a shuffle feel. Notice the similarities between this tune and the other blues tunes you have just learned. Many forms of American popular music are somehow related to the blues. Make a list of as many songs as you can think of that have this "blues sound" and discuss them with the class.

PERFORMANCE SPOTLIGHT

 **Alert** This tune contains 1st and 2nd endings (page 36), except here they are 1st – 7th endings. Just keep repeating the first bracketed ending six times, then finish with the 7th ending.

Play the accompaniment to this Hank Williams tune with a power chord shuffle. Shuffles in music are often indicated by ($\square = \overline{\square \; \square}$) at the beginning of the song.

127. MOVE IT ON OVER

Hank Williams

1. Came in last night at half past ten. That ba-by of mine— would-n't
2.–7. See additional verses below

let me in,—— so move it on o-ver. (Move it on o-ver.)

Move it on o-ver. (Move it on o-ver.) Move o-ver, lit-tle dog,— 'cause the

big dog's— mov-in'—— in.——

2. She's

2. She's changed the lock on our front door
   And my door key don't fit no more.
   So get it on over. (Move it on over.) Scoot it on over. (Move it on over.)
   Move over, skinny dog, 'cause the fat dog's movin' in.

3. This dog house here is mighty small
   But it's better than no house at all.
   So ease it on over. (Move it on over.) Drag it on over. (Move it on over.)
   Move over, old dog, 'cause a new dog's movin' in.

4. She told me not to play around,
   But I done let the deal go down.
   So pack it on over. (Move it on over.) Tote it on over. (Move it on over.)
   Move over, nice dog, 'cause a mad dog's movin' in.

5. She warned me once, she warned me twice,
   But I don't take no one's advice.
   So scratch it on over. (Move it on over.) Shake it on over. (Move it on over.)
   Move over, short dog, 'cause a tall dog's movin' in.

6. She'll crawl back to me on her knees.
   I'll be busy scratchin' fleas.
   So slide it on over. (Move it on over.) Sneak it on over. (Move it on over.)
   Move over, good dog, 'cause a mad dog's movin' in.

7. Remember pup, before you whine,
   That side's yours and this side's mine.
   So shove it on over. (Move it on over.) Sweep it on over. (Move it on over.)
   Move over, cold dog, 'cause a hot dog's movin' in.

PERFORMANCE SPOTLIGHT

STRUM BUILDER 10

Practice these new strum patterns and use them on the following tune.

128. SIMPLE STRUM 1

129. SIMPLE STRUM 2

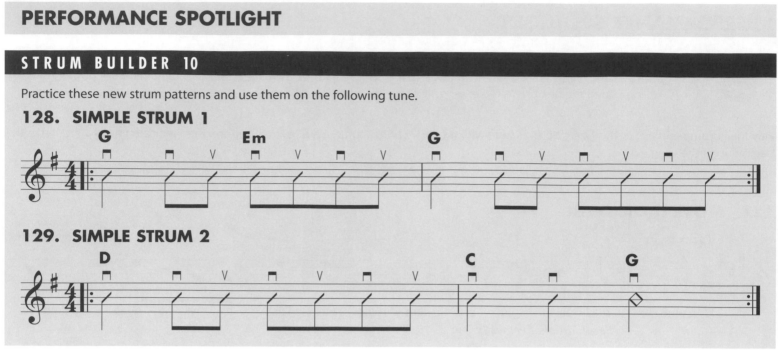

Play "Simple Gifts" as a duet with a friend or teacher using the melody (Gtr. 1) and the harmony line (Gtr. 2). Add another person to play the chord accompaniment (using the strum patterns above) for a trio.

130. SIMPLE GIFTS

Traditional Shaker Hymn

NEW NOTES

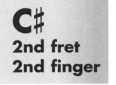

C#
2nd fret
2nd finger

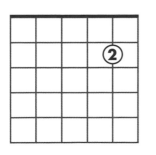

C#

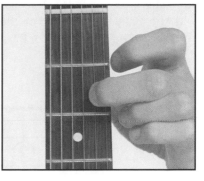

The following tune is a great exercise in rhythm. The notes are few and fairly easy (including the new C#), but the rhythms can get tricky. The key to playing this song correctly is counting the rests carefully. Review the eighth rest (page 74) and syncopation (page 30) to help in understanding these rhythms. Count and clap through the song first before playing.

131. LOW RIDER

Sylvester Allen, Harold R. Brown, Morris Dickerson, Jerry Goldstein,
Leroy Jordan, Lee Oskar, Charles W. Miller & Howard Scott

PLAYING CHORDS

B7 is your first four-finger chord. Notice that the finger formation used on strings 3–5 is the same as is used on strings 1–3 of the D7 chord, with the pinky finger added on the first string, 2nd fret. Keeping this familiar D7 chord shape in mind will help you move to the B7 chord quickly. The bass string for B7 is the fifth string.

B7 Chord

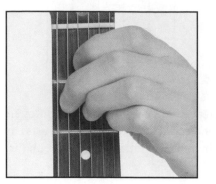

Try out the B7 chord in the Woody Guthrie tune below. When you change from E to B7, keep the 2nd finger down. Use the bass/strum $\frac{3}{4}$ pattern or the p-i-m-a-m-i finger pick from "Time is on My Side" (page 66).

132. RAMBLIN' ROUND

Woodie Guthrie, Huddie Ledbetter & John Lomax

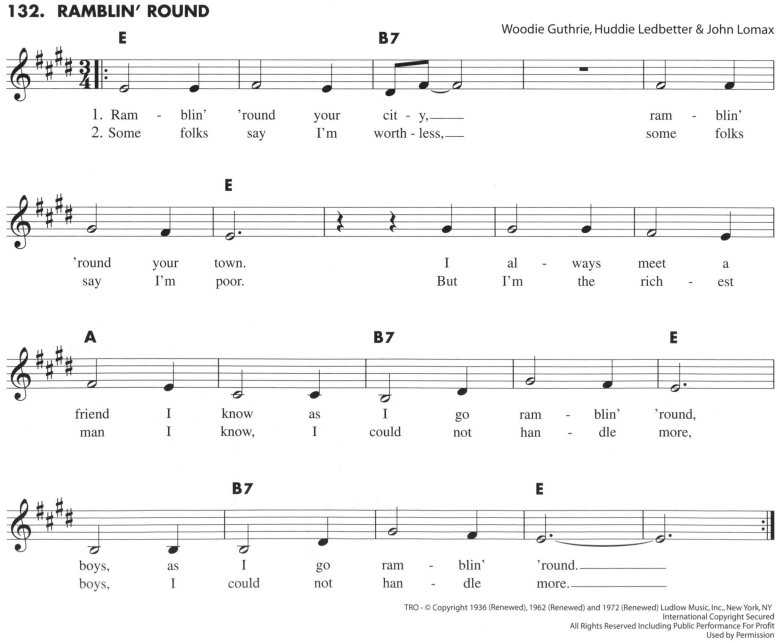

1. Ram - blin' 'round your cit - y,_____ ram - blin'
2. Some folks say I'm worth - less,_____ some folks

'round your town. I al - ways meet a
say I'm poor. But I'm the rich - est

friend I know as I go ram - blin' 'round,
man I know, I could not han - dle more,

boys, as I go ram - blin' 'round._____
boys, I could not han - dle more._____

PLAYING CHORDS

There are two ways of playing the E7 chord: either as a subtraction from or an addition to the E chord that you already know.
The four-finger version is preferable if you are finger picking. The bass string for E7 is the open sixth string.

E7
Chord

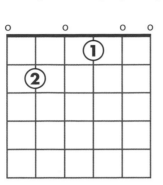

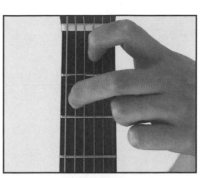

E7
Chord

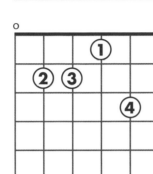

The next song is a 12-bar blues using the new E7 and B7 chords. Play with a shuffle feel.

133. GOOD MORNIN' BLUES

Huddie Ledbetter & Alan Lomax

1. Good morn-in' blues,— blues how do you do?_____ Good
2., 3. Additional verses below

morn-in' blues,— blues how do you do?_____ I'm

do-in' al-right, good morn-in' how are you?—— 1., 2. Lay 3. The

2. Lay down last night, tryin' to take my rest,
   Lay down last night, tryin' to take my rest.
   My mind kept ramblin' like the wild geese in the west.

3. The sun gonna shine on my back door some day,
   The sun gonna shine on my back door some day.
   The wind gonna rise up and blow my blues away.

PERFORMANCE SPOTLIGHT

HISTORY

Johann Sebastian Bach (1685–1750), the famous German composer and organist, wrote over 1000 classical compositions in his lifetime. He came from a very musical family and had several sons who went on to become famous composers/musicians as well. Bach himself didn't become very well-known until after his death, but his incredible music legacy lives on strong hundreds of years later.

Learn each part of the following Bach piece and play it with a friend or teacher. Play the chord accompaniment as well using the bass/strum ¾ pattern. You may also finger pick the accompaniment with p - $\frac{a}{m}$ - $\frac{a}{m}$ (pick the three fingers as a unit on beats 2 and 3).

134. MINUET IN G

J. S. Bach

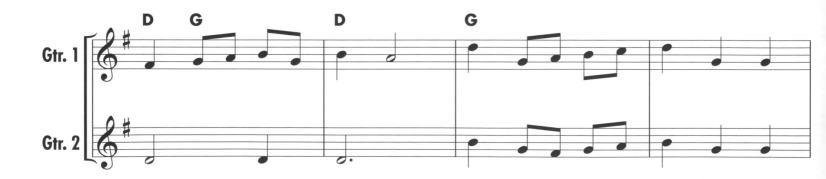

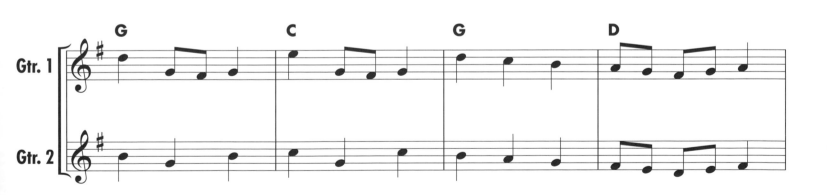

PERFORMANCE SPOTLIGHT

HISTORY

Huddie Ledbetter (1885–1949), better known as "Leadbelly," was the "King of the 12-String Guitar." Some of his best-known songs include "Goodnight Irene," "Rock Island Line," and "Cotton Fields."

135. MIDNIGHT SPECIAL *Sing and strum this prison song with a shuffle feel.*

Prison Song

Well you wake up in the morn - ing,—— hear the ding - dong ring.—— Go march-ing to the ta - ble,—— see the same darn thing. Knife and fork are on the ta - ble—— noth-in' in my pan,—— and if you say a thing a - bout it,—— you're in trou - ble with the

Chorus

man. Let the mid-night spe - cial,—— shine its light on you.—— Let the mid-night spe - cial—— shine its ev - er lov-in' light on you.

Copyright © 2005 by HAL LEONARD CORPORATION
International Copyright Secured All Rights Reserved

136. ESSENTIAL CREATIVITY

Play "Midnight Special" again using the power chord shuffle (page 77 and 78). Then try playing the power chords with an even eighth-note rhythm.

HISTORY

12-string guitars are variations of the standard 6-string guitar. They have the same six strings as the standard 6-string, but with each string doubled, creating a broader, fuller sound. The lowest four strings are doubled with strings an octave higher, while the highest two strings are doubled with strings of the same octave.

PERFORMANCE SPOTLIGHT

Practice both parts of the following duet. You can play Gtr. 1 alone as a solo, or play Gtr. 1 and 2 as a duet with a friend or teacher. Record yourself playing the chord accompaniment or one of the written parts and then play a duet with yourself.

137. RONDEAU

Jean-Joseph Mouret

PLAYING CHORDS

Barre	Certain guitar chords require you to **barre** a finger across more than one string. This involves fretting several strings with one finger by depressing with the side of the finger instead of with just the fingertip.

Unlike other chords you have played, the F chord has two strings depressed by one finger. The index finger barres across strings 1 and 2. You will find that it is easier to roll this finger slightly so that the strings are depressed by the outside rather than the flat underside of the 1st finger. The barre is shown with a curved line in the chord diagram below. The bass note for F is on the fourth string.

F
Chord

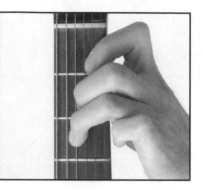

Play both finger picking and strumming for this next song that includes the F chord. Also play the melody once you've learned the chords.

138. JINGLE BELLS

J. Pierpont

continue finger picking throughout

Verse

Chorus

139. ESSENTIAL ELEMENTS QUIZ *Name the notes shown below. Try naming the chords on the second line as well.*

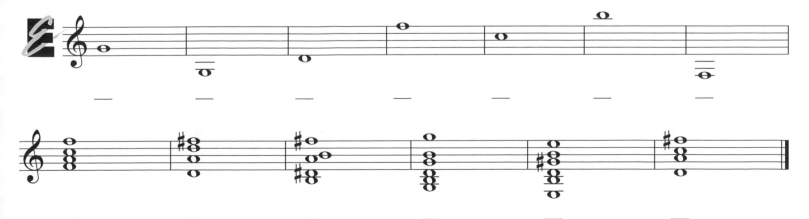

PERFORMANCE SPOTLIGHT

Fermata   Also known as a "bird's eye," a **fermata** (𝄐) is a symbol in notation used to indicate a hold (or pause) in the music. The duration of the held note or rest is typically decided by the player (or conductor). A fermata is marked above the note or rest to be held.

140. THE STAR SPANGLED BANNER *Play the melody and chords to America's National Anthem.*

Francis Scott Key & John Stafford Smith

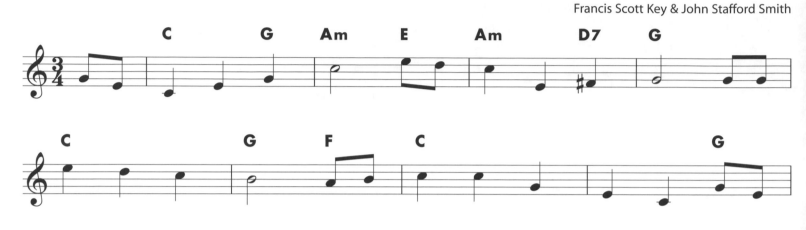

PERFORMANCE SPOTLIGHT

HISTORY

The 1964 rock 'n' roll song, "You Really Got Me" by **The Kinks**, was re-recorded by the rock group **Van Halen** in 1978. The now-famous guitar player of the group, Eddie Van Halen, created a new guitar technique known as *finger tapping*, which involves the use of both hands on the fretboard simultaneously. "You Really Got Me," and particularly the guitar solo "Eruption," both from Van Halen's popular self-titled 1978 album, showcase Eddie's mesmerizing technique.

141. YOU REALLY GOT ME *Play the melody of this rock anthem.*

Ray Davies

OTHER TUNING METHODS

Electronic Tuners

An electronic tuner "reads" the pitch of a sound and tells you whether or not the pitch is correct. Until your ear is well trained in hearing pitches, this can be a much more accurate way to tune.

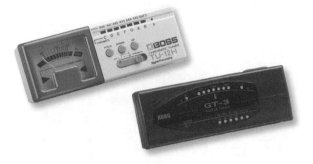

Keyboard

If you have a piano or keyboard nearby, play the correct key (see diagram) and slowly turn the corresponding tuning key until the sound of the string matches the sound of the keyboard.

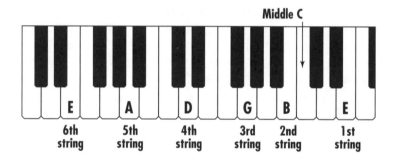

Relative Tuning

To check or correct your tuning when no pitch source is available, you can use relative tuning, in which the strings are tuned relative to one another. Follow these steps:

- Assume that the sixth string is tuned correctly to E.

- Press the sixth string at the 5th fret. This is the pitch A to which you tune your open fifth string. Play the depressed sixth string and the fifth string with your thumb. When the two sounds match, you are in tune.

- Press the fifth string at the 5th fret and tune the open fourth string to it. Follow the same procedure that you did on the fifth and sixth strings.

- Press the fourth string at the 5th fret and tune the open third string to it.

- To tune the second string, press the third string at the 4th fret and tune the open second string to it.

- Press the second string at the 5th fret and tune the first string to it.

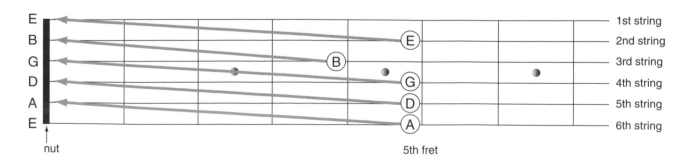

REFERENCE INDEX

Definitions (pg.)

CHORD CHART

Instrument Care

Some basic tips on keeping your instrument in good working condition:

- Wipe down the strings with a dry cloth every time you are done playing; this will increase string life.

- Never keep your guitar in the car or outside overnight; extreme temperatures could cause extreme damage to your instrument.

- Store your instrument in a room-temperature environment.

- If your guitar is cold from being transported outside, allow it to warm up in a room-temperature environment in its case first before playing.

C
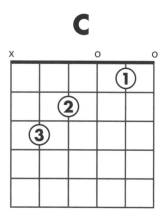

G7
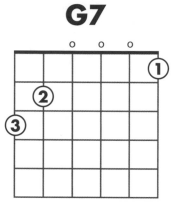

G
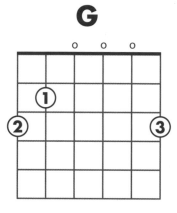

D7
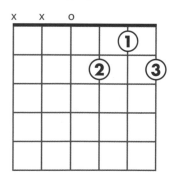

Em
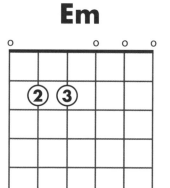

D
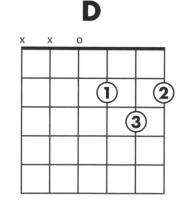

A7
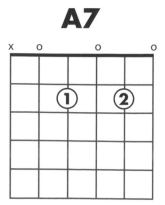

Em7
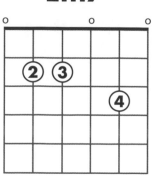

Em7
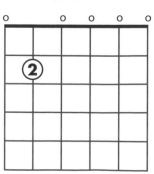

Am

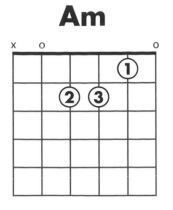

Am7

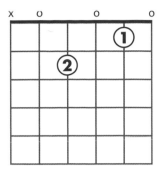

A

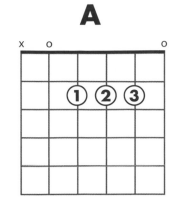

Dm

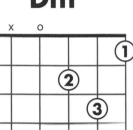

E

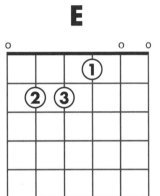

E5

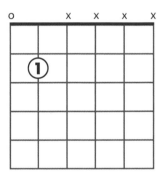

A5

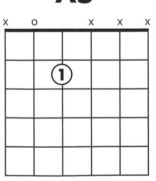

D5

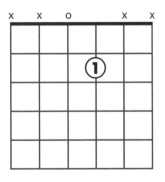

B7

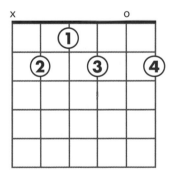

E7

E7

F

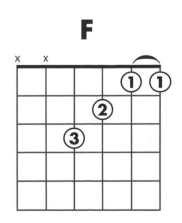

PRACTICE RECORD

Week	Date	Assignment/Exercises	Mon	Tue	Wed	Thurs	Fri	Sat	Sun	Total	Parent Initials
1											
2											
3											
4											
5											
6											
7											
8											
9											
10											
11											
12											
13											
14											
15											
16											
17											
18											
19											
20											
21											
22											
23											
24											
25											
26											
27											
28											
29											
30											
31											
32											
33											
34	Date	Assignment/Exercises	Mon	Tue	Wed	Thurs	Fri	Sat	Sun	Total	Parent Initials
35											
36											